Mary Quite Contrary

Mary Quite Contrary

◆

The Story of a Lion-Hearted Mom Raising a Bipolar Daughter

Gayle Carson Lagman-Creswick

iUniverse, Inc.
New York Lincoln Shanghai

Mary Quite Contrary
The Story of a Lion-Hearted Mom Raising a Bipolar Daughter

iUniverse books may be ordered through booksellers or by contacting:

iUniverse
2021 Pine Lake Road, Suite 100
Lincoln, NE 68512
www.iuniverse.com
1-800-Authors (1-800-288-4677)

Because of the dynamic nature of the Internet, any Web addresses or links contained in this book may have changed since publication and may no longer be valid.

The views expressed in this work are solely those of the author and do not necessarily reflect the views of the publisher, and the publisher hereby disclaims any responsibility for them.

ISBN: 978-0-595-44076-4 (pbk)
ISBN: 978-0-595-68943-9 (cloth)
ISBN: 978-0-595-88399-8 (ebk)

Printed in the United States of America

This book is dedicated to Mary Quite Contrary ... who did not choose to have Bipolar Disorder.

Mary, Mary quite contrary,
Why did you act up so?
You had Bipolar Disorder, it seems;
So sorry we did not know ...

Contents

Introduction

This is a true story of the Lagman family. I am Gayle, the mother. I grew up in the rural Colorado town of Wray, became a registered nurse and married Raul, a Filipino doctor. I later received a bachelor's degree in psychology and went on to have a successful career as an executive and consultant in the healthcare and retirement industry. Our sons were Steve, Matt, Mike, and Bruce. Our daughters, Mary and Kim, were adopted after our boys were born. Mary and Kim were not biological sisters. They were very close in age, only two months apart. Mary was adopted at eight days old and Kim at age two. At age forty-seven I found myself raising a grandchild, Mary's son Andrew, who became my seventh child.

The Lagman family life and marriage experienced the normal stresses of a big family, plus the added stress of two special needs daughters and later the pressures brought on by marital conflict, divorce, and two demanding careers. I wanted it all. I wanted a big family, a successful career, volunteer work, and on and on. I wanted to hold the world close.

This book is about unconditional love. You may not pick that up at first, because it is about hard-core love ... that knock-me-down-and-I-will-get-right-back-up-and-love-you kind of love. Anyone can love a beautiful, bright, well-behaved child. It takes tenacity, determination, and the patience of Job to continue loving a child who exhibits bad behavior daily; a child who does about everything possible to convince you not to love her. The book is also about walking a tightrope ... balancing a stressful career with the demands of home. It is about providing the care and nourishment of four healthy kids while tending to the special needs of the other two. It is also about a home where emotions run high and at any minute, eruptions can occur which change a perfectly-sunshiny day into a tornado.

Mary Quite Contrary is a book about living with Bipolar Disorder, although we did not know for many years that Mary, in fact, had Bipolar Disorder. That is often the case with this disorder. First, you come to believe you are a bad parent, then you begin to think something is wrong with the child, but it is a long time before anyone is willing to put a name on it.

According to the National Institute of Mental Health there are about 20.9 million people who are diagnosed with Bipolar Disorder which is categorized as a mood disorder. I believe there are millions more who go undiagnosed, at least for a good part of their life. I suspect our prisons are full of undiagnosed bipolar people. I can only imagine the broken marriages, dysfunctional families, addictions, and other problems caused by the disorder … especially by those undiagnosed and untreated.

Some of the names in this story have been changed in order to preserve dignity and trust. I purposely did not go into our other adopted daughter Kim's story because that would be too much for one book. So keep in mind as you read along, that we adopted two girls whose lives were forever changed by biological mothers who chose to use drugs during their pregnancies. We loved them when we adopted them, and we will always love them. They did not ask for these troubles. They are our daughters and sisters forever, and we would not have it any other way.

Many who read this story will feel frustration with me for keeping the relationship going with Mary in spite of the pain. To me, unconditional love means that you do not give up on a loved one until "death do us part."

If the telling of certain events inadvertently hurts individuals, it was never the intent. I related events as *I* lived and perceived them. I invited other family members to write their observations and perceptions. Some chose to write and some did not. I have learned that there are as many facets to family dynamics as there are family members.

1

Taking a Stand

The next time fourteen-year-old Mary goes over the line I will call the police. How can I call the police on my own daughter? I'm not sure I can. My older boys are afraid someone in this family is going to get hurt if I don't do something. Calling the police sounds like a last resort. I am a single mom who cannot handle my own daughter.

I always thought I was a good parent. I have loved all of my kids dearly and I felt sure they all knew it ... with the exception of Mary. For whatever reason she would frequently declare that she was not loved. How can you raise all your kids with the same standards and doses of love and yet they do not respond to it in the same way? The boys seemed to thrive on that recipe. The problems with Mary were causing me to rethink whether or not I was a good parent. *What is a good parent anyway?*

Mary soon provided me with the reason to make that police call. She called me at work. "I'm going to the mall with a friend and I need some money."

I explained, "Mary, you've already spent your money." She hung up on me after firing bad-word bullets into my ear. When I arrived home at 5:30 P.M. all the doors were locked and chained, and she refused to let me in. I tried pleading, then demanding for about forty-five minutes. Then I felt so disgusted that I turned around, drove up to the Circle K, and called the police. "My teen-age daughter has locked me out of the house. I need your help," I told the police dispatcher, who was kind to me and did not ask many questions. I felt like crying. I felt nauseated. *It has come to this.*

"We will be right out," the dispatcher said.

There. I did it. I called the police on my own daughter. My hands were shaking so that I could hardly drive the car. Many of my friends and family had told me that I should take action and call the police. It wasn't easy. I met them at the house. There were two of them. Officer Thorne was a big, black guy; about six foot four, with broad shoulders. He beat his fist on the door and yelled, "Mesa Police Department, open this door!" He repeated it three times before Mary finally opened the door. The other male officer stood by and let Thorne handle things.

Mary called out to me, "You fucking bitch, why did you call the cops?" She proceeded to walk back to her bedroom. The big guy was right after her. He sat down on the bed beside her. I watched from the hallway.

"Young lady you have a bad mouth on you. And what do you mean locking your mother out of the house? You don't own this house. Your mother does." His booming voice would have scared most people. Not Mary, at least that she showed. "Talking like that is going to get you nothing but trouble," he warned her.

"I don't care. She's a bitch."

"Why did you lock your mother out of the house?" he asked.

"It's none of your business!"

"Let me tell you something, young lady; if you keep this up, you're going to land yourself in jail. Is that what you want?"

"Who cares? I sure don't," she said.

"All I can tell you is that you *better* care. You need to clean up your act; no more locking your mother out of the house," he said, as he walked away from her. "I don't want to get another call like this."

I walked them to the door. As Thorpe passed by me he was shaking his head as he said, "Lady, you have your hands full with that girl. Good luck." I wished I could adopt Officer Thorne; if he lived in this house, I felt Mary would shape-up fast.

After that episode I felt hopeful. I had called her bluff. She would think twice about doing something like that again. Wrong. It didn't seem to faze her. The police and I became so well known to each other that we addressed each other by first names. Sometimes, when I called the police they would say, "Is that Mary acting up again?" If they didn't know Mary, many of them knew *of* her from their fellow workers. She was well known within the local police department ... not something I was proud to admit.

In fact, I was dreadfully ashamed. These problems did not seem to go with my respectable job and otherwise respectable family. *Was this snob talk? Maybe. Some-one with my education ought to be able to correct this problem. I desperately want to solve this problem. If only I could wave a magic wand and take it all away. I yearn for normalcy, although I don't remember what normal is. I feel as if I have been dragged into a disturbing movie that I didn't want to see in the first place. I want to leave this movie, but I can't. I am forty-three years old; shouldn't my life be getting easier?*

From somewhere the answer came, "You are it, kid; this is the hand you have been dealt. Play it."

I heard about a program called "Tough Love" and decided to attend a support group on Monday evening. I arrived home, prepared supper, and told Bruce, Mary and Kim that I was going to a meeting. Mary was upset with me because she wanted me to take her somewhere. "Mary, I'm going to a meeting. It's important." I explained.

"You're not going anywhere," she said.

"What do you mean?" I asked.

"You're just not," and she left the kitchen.

I was busy preparing our meal and forgot all about it until Kim came into the kitchen and said, "Mom, Mary took your car."

"What?"

"She took the keys and left," Kim said.

"She's only fourteen years old, and she thinks she knows how to drive? She will crash!" I ran outside and looked up and down the street, hoping she had just moved the car. No Mary. I heard a siren and feared she might have been in an accident. I said a frantic prayer. "God, please don't let that siren be about Mary."

I called the police immediately. Three officers, two men and one woman, responded very fast. They must have been nearby. They came into the house, and I angrily explained that Mary had been acting out because she did not get her way, and now she had taken my car. I could tell by the scowls on their faces that they disapproved of my anger. They were obviously not officers who were familiar with Mary's many shenanigans.

I vented on them. "I've had it. I needed to go to a meeting tonight, and she took my car so I couldn't go. She should be arrested. Can you put her in jail? She needs to know she cannot do this."

The young female officer looked surprised at my comment and said, "You know, Mary is *your* responsibility. You can't just run off to a meeting when she needs you."

I looked the officer in the eye and said, "You have no idea what I have been through with her. I was going to a "Tough Love" meeting tonight to learn how to better deal with her."

"You know, Mrs. Lagman, some of these tough love groups think that it's okay to shirk your responsibility as a parent," she said.

Frustrated, I inquired of this young, rosy-cheeked female officer, "Do you have any children?"

"No, I'm not married," she said.

"I hope you never have to deal with a child like this," I said to her sincerely. "I thought I knew how to handle kids after being the youngest of twelve children myself, and then the mother of six. I also had eighteen foster children, some of whom had problems. I'm also a nurse and I even have a degree in psychology … none of which have prepared me for handling Mary."

At that time, about thirty minutes into her joy ride, Mary pulled into the driveway. I looked at my watch; it was 7:15 P.M. If I hurried I could still make the meeting. I desperately needed it.

"Mrs. Lagman, let's sit down and discuss this with Mary." The young female officer said.

"I'm sorry. I can't talk to Mary right now. The best thing I can do is go to this meeting. If you want to talk to her, be my guest." My voice was still filled with anger. I took the keys, ran out to the car and left. *That female officer thinks I'm a witch. I think she is still wet behind the ears. She thinks I'm a lousy mother and I think she is a green cop. She is leaping to conclusions without knowing the situation. I don't care what she thinks. I am going to this meeting.*

They did not arrest Mary. She was sound asleep when I arrived home at 9:30 P.M. Mary often manipulated officers, especially the ones who didn't know her. She could be very convincing, even charming, when she wanted. In fact, Mary was a charming person about twenty percent of the time. It was the other 80% that gave us trouble. She must have been operating on her 20% this time.

I learned from my tough love meeting to keep saying no and not to give in to Mary. Once she knew the rules and did not follow them, we were to stick to the consequence. If she still ignored the rule, then we should kick her out of our house and refer her to another tough love home, where she should stay until she agreed to follow the rules. It sounded good, but they didn't know Mary. She would not stay at another house. She would break their doors down or burn their house down. She would go to any extreme not to be corralled. Even when she was four years old she hated obstacles such as a "time-out" given as a form of discipline. More than once she jumped out a second story window during a time-out. When I would go to release her from the time-out, she was not there.

Mary was not always raging. On rare occasions she would climb in bed with me, give me a hug and say tearfully, "Mama, I love you. Please don't give up on me. You are the only one who believes in me." It was during those moments I fully realized I would never stop loving her or believing in her. Inside her was a special person. I knew it. *If only I could find the key.*

I would hug her and reassure her, "No matter what, I will not give up on you. I don't like some of the things you do, but I always love you." I had learned in my psych classes that it was important to separate the doer from the deed. In other words, you can still love the child but not the behavior. Sometimes it was awfully hard to separate them.

The next day after she voiced her love for me, it was as if she had never let down her defenses. *Did that really happen last night? Did she really come into my bed and ask me not to give up on her? Did I dream it? Where is that soft and loving person?*

There were times when Mary was so enjoyable that I would almost forget all the problems. I wondered why she could not be that way all the time. She had a good sense of humor and we had some good laughs together. I cherished those times and they gave me hope for how it *could* be.

Mary seemed to define love in terms of material goods. If she were given "stuff," she felt loved. When she heard "no," and did not receive material goods, it seemed as if she felt unloved, and then she would tailspin. I thought this was a carry-over from her dad giving in to her demands and lavishing her with money and whatever else she wanted. I tried to figure out how to get her to see that love and material goods were not connected.

"Mary, when your dad gave you money and bought you things you wanted, you felt loved. Now you feel if you do not receive the things you want, you are not loved. Love has nothing to do with money or gifts. It has to do with caring … sometimes caring enough to say 'no.' I love you, but I will not play that game of giving things to you so you feel loved," I explained. "If I do that, you will never get it straight." She did not appear to grasp it. It didn't help.

After I gave in to summoning the police, I had my first taste of what humility was all about. I had always cared too much what people thought about me. Is that pride? False pride? After a police incident, I felt embarrassed to face my neighbors, wondering what they thought. For one thing, they didn't know me. I had only lived in this house for one year. They must have thought they were living next door to "low lives." I made a mental note not to judge others by what their kids did. Or, for that matter, do not judge them period. I had been guilty of thinking police intervention meant that parents weren't doing their job. Mary may not have learned anything so far, but I was learning humility. I was also learning to feel compassion for other families with troubled kids. When my employees at work had trouble with their kids, I understood what they were going through.

I was beginning to feel more and more hopeless about the situation with Mary. For whatever reason, her behavior was accelerating. *Is this adolescence? Is she getting worse because her dad is not here to give in to her? What is causing this increase in bad behaviors? How far will it go?*

We tried counseling again, which I was not hopeful about, because Mary would not listen or cooperate. In the first place, she said she did not believe she had a problem. The counselor ended up saying she couldn't help because Mary refused to cooperate.

The relationship between Mary and me became a power struggle of the highest order. If I said no, she said yes. If I said something was black, she said it was white. She swore that nothing was wrong with her. "You're the ones who have a problem," she said over and over.

It reminded me of the movie *High Noon* where a little old wacky lady was on the witness stand and she said, "Everyone is pixilated, except me."

One day Mary and her sister Kim (who was the same age as Mary) were watching an after school TV program on adoption. They both knew they were adopted and we had told them what we knew about their biological parents. After the program Mary had lots of questions about her biological family, but I did not have enough information to answer all of them. She was very curious about whom she looked like in her bio family, and if she had any "real" (Mary's word) brothers and sisters. I said to her, "If the day comes when you want to try to find them, I will help you." Mary actually looked as if she were our biological child. She looked like our boys who were Asian-American. Their father was Filipino and I Caucasian. Kim and I were the fair-skinned ones in the family.

After that TV special, Mary would often say in the middle of a rage, "I don't belong to this family. I don't fit in. I belong to another family. They are the ones I belong to. Why did you have to adopt me? I should be with them." I took it personally when she said this stuff. It hurt. Obviously, Mary had no idea how much I loved her. I learned that it didn't matter how much you loved a child. If the child perceived that you did not love him or her, *that* was the reality with which you had to deal.

2

Never On Sunday

A certain Sunday night would be forever etched in my memory. Mary had a friend Nancy for an overnight, and they wanted to sleep in the addition so they could use the sauna. The addition was part of our house, but you had to go outside and in through an arcadia door to get there, or else go through the garage. I said it was okay. About 10:30 P.M. the two girls came in and asked, "Could we go for a walk?"

"No," I said. "It's too late, and besides it is not safe for you to be out." Mary begged for a little while and then backed off, which was uncommon.

About 11:00 P.M. I went out to the addition to check on them. They were not there. Evidently they had gone over the back wall. I was mad and worried. *Why is it that kids seem to have no conception of how their parents worry about their safety?* When Mary acted out I often needed help to bring her back. I awakened Bruce and Kim to help look for Mary and Nancy. I also felt responsible for Nancy. I was sure her parents trusted that I would look after Nancy when she was at our house. We drove around the neighborhood until midnight. We were almost back home when we saw Mary and Nancy walking toward home. "Get in the car. We are taking Nancy home. You disobeyed me, so Nancy cannot spend the night. I called her parents and told them what you've done. They know we are bringing Nancy home."

Mary was livid and spewed four-letter words at me all the way to her friend's house. In fact, her behavior was so bad, I wondered if they had gotten into drugs or alcohol. I couldn't smell any alcohol. When we arrived home, she headed out into the addition. I said, "You need to come into the house and into your own bedroom to sleep. What is going on anyway? Did you take something?"

"That's a stupid question. No, I didn't take anything, and I'm not coming in."

"Yes, you are," I insisted.

"No, I am not!"

After seeing that we were at a stand-off, I ran to get sixteen-year-old Bruce. "Bruce, she is coming inside if we have to bodily pick her up and bring her in," I told him. By this time I was out of patience.

Bruce, also filled with disgust by this time, ran out there and said, "Come on, Mary. Get inside. It's late! What are you trying to pull?" As he approached her, she pulled out from under the bed two big butcher knives, one in each hand, and started waving them at Bruce.

"Come on tough guy; see how brave you are now," she threatened, all the time waving those butcher knives back and forth in front of him.

Bruce started to go after her and I said quickly, "Bruce! Come on! Leave her alone. It's not worth it." There was no doubt in my mind that she would cut him with the knives if he did not back off. Mary was out of control.

We ducked into the house. She locked the arcadia door after us and pulled the drapery closed. We could see through a tiny crack where the drapery did not come together. She was hollering like a crazy person. We couldn't hear everything, but we heard her saying, "You are all going to be sorry. I will finish you off. When I light this candle, you're going to burn! I hate all of you!"

Bruce and I looked at each other with alarm at what she might do next. *What is she up to? Has she lost her mind?* We peeked through the crack. We could smell gasoline. We saw her with the lawn mower gas can, apparently scattering gas around the perimeter of the room like a wild woman.

I ran to the kitchen phone and dialed 911. "I need help. My daughter has locked herself in a room attached to our house and has scattered gasoline around. She says she has a candle and is going to burn us up. You must get here right away, but please don't blow sirens; if she hears you coming, she will light the candle." Mary was like some animals who, when cornered, become aggressive.

"You need to go outside, away from the house, and wait for us. Right now!" the dispatcher cautioned. We ran outside, and within a few minutes the emergency vehicles began arriving quietly. It felt scary and strange, like watching a television drama unfold. There were two hook and ladder trucks and four police cars.

One of the officers who knew Mary said to me, "Mary has no idea that she has created a bomb in there. If she lights that candle the fumes will cause an explosion. You need to take your family and go down the street. We are going to evacuate your neighbors too." I opened the garage for them. Inside the garage was the second door into the addition where Mary was holed up. It was eerily quiet outside. Inside Mary was ranting and raving at the top of her voice.

We began walking down the street, Kim, Bruce and I, with our arms around each other, scared to death. I was crying out of fear for what might happen. I realized that I was not worried about the house. I was afraid that Mary would blow herself up. I was also concerned that the officers would get hurt. If she lit that candle she would not be the only one hurt. We comforted each other the best we could, mostly we just hooked eyes with each other and shook our heads, sharing disbelief that this could be happening to us. I could only imagine the trauma to Kim and Bruce. Kim was fourteen and Bruce was sixteen. Bruce said, "I can't believe Mary has gone this far. It's unbelievable. What is wrong with her?"

"I wish I knew," I said.

After a half hour of suspense, we were summoned back to the house by one of the officers. "It's over. No one is hurt, except one of our officers got nicked with a butcher knife." The officer related the details to us, "I thought I could talk Mary out of there, because she knew me from school, and we had a pretty good relationship. I almost had her out. She opened the door with the lit candle in her hand and saw all the officers. She started to slam the door, but we zapped her with the fire hose, put the candle out and subdued her. It was a close call. We have her in the police car. I'm afraid you have a lot of water in that room. We are taking Mary in. She wants to talk with you. She is in the back seat of my car over there," he pointed.

I went over to the squad car where Mary was handcuffed in the back seat. "Mom," she cried, "Please don't let them put me in jail. Please, please, please, Mom! I'm sorry," she sobbed and pleaded.

"It's out of my hands now, Mary. What you did was very serious," I said. "It is a police matter now." It broke my heart to see those handcuffs on her. I knew she was sorry. She was always sorry after a near catastrophe and she seemed sincere. *If only Mary could open her eyes before it comes to this. Will this event open her eyes? It dawns on me that jail is not what she needs. She needs psychiatric care, so someone can figure out what is wrong with her. How can I get her into a psych hospital? Where is all this going to end?*

The firemen helped us clean up some of the water mess. I sent Bruce and Kim to bed. I felt bone tired and my knees were like jelly, I guess from the fright of the whole thing. It was 3:00 A.M. when I finally got to bed. I replayed the evening's events over and over in my head. *She could have killed us all tonight. We cannot go on like this.*

What will it take to help this child? Where have I gone wrong as a parent? I reviewed my present situation. *I have two lives ... my successful life at work and my struggles at home. I have something like a light switch, which I switch on and off.*

When I arrive at work, I switch off home. When I arrive home, I turn off work. I use the ten minute drive between the two to do the switching. Tomorrow at work I will have a busy day without any sleep tonight. I prayed for Mary and tried to imagine her in a jail cell. *Is she sleeping? Is she in a cell by herself? Jail sounds foreign to me. Has anyone I know been in jail? This is new territory and I don't like it. I remember a little line I wrote in Creative Writing: "Why is it that reality is always more than I want?"*

The next day, when driving home from work, I drove past my house three times. Bruce and Kim happened to be watching out the big window and saw me go by again and again. I finally made the turn into our driveway. "What's up Mom? You passed our house three times!" They were laughing.

"Sometimes it takes me a while to switch over from work to home," I told them. They probably thought I was just plain goofy.

I thought a lot about Mary in jail. I didn't feel that jail was the right place for her. I didn't have enough money for intensive psychiatric intervention. We had worked our way through the school counselors and through counseling at Tri-City Mental Health. Not one counselor mentioned the possibility of bipolar mood disorder or any other disorder for that matter. I felt she needed to be hospitalized, but how could I make that happen? I made some phone calls. The admissions people explained to me that hospitalization was only for acute situations. To them Mary did not appear to be acutely mentally ill. I asked them what their definition of acute was. They were evasive. Anyway, they had a waiting list for a bed. I wondered how many people who really needed psychiatric help were placed in jails and prisons. It seemed to me that if kids went untreated, they eventually made their way into jail. I read that Arizona was number fifty in the U.S. for spending on mental health programs. I didn't know where to turn for help.

After experiencing crisis after crisis, I developed a kind of amnesia as a defense mechanism. The week after an event, like the gasoline incident, I had trouble remembering the sequence of the events, or sometimes I couldn't remember what caused the incident. I read that amnesia was a common defense mechanism with events such as these. If I remembered in detail every single crisis with Mary it would probably drive me nuts. Mary's description of what had happened was always different from my memory of it. She often said, "I never said that." or "I never did that." Perhaps that was *her* defense mechanism.

Most of the time I was still determined to find the key to turning Mary around. Sometimes I was so weary of it all, that I could only vegetate. Sometimes I wanted to go to bed, pull the covers over my head and stay there forever. There had to be a key. Could I find it? I felt sorry for Kim and Bruce. Mary demanded so much of my attention that often there wasn't much of me left for them. They did not complain, at least out loud. Sometimes Bruce would say, "What is wrong with her? What makes her act this way? Why can't she see what she's doing? Is she just spoiled rotten?"

As a result of the near house fire, Mary spent some time in juvenile detention hall and then was given probation. A probation officer named Bob was assigned to her case. We met with him. He was a nice-looking guy in his upper twenties. Bob seemed to get along with Mary and we liked him. He seemed genuinely interested in turning Mary around. I told him that I felt Mary needed to be hospitalized. He said, "Juvenile hall is filled with kids who need psychiatric care, but get jail instead."

Great. Our country can afford to care for people in jails and prisons, but they cannot afford prevention in the form of psychiatric care. I felt hopeless. Hopelessness was getting to be my constant companion. *How did I get to this point? What happened to my beautiful baby girl? She has turned into someone I don't know. Where have I gone wrong? What am I going to do now? Where are you, God? What have I done to deserve this? It all started out so well. How did I arrive at this point? Did I do something to cause these problems with Mary? Was it something in my childhood that caused me not to be able to solve these problems?*

3

The Decision to Adopt

I am Gayle, the mother of Mary. I grew up the youngest of twelve children in Wray, Colorado. My parents homesteaded in the sand hills just outside of town. Wray, a town of about 2500, was a town of salt-of-the-earth people. When a Wrayite met you on the street and asked how you were, they really wanted to know. When tragedy struck a Wray family, the people rallied around. I always thought of it as my town and I still do.

I had as carefree and happy existence as a child could have. As the baby of a family made up of nine boys and three girls (two boys and a girl died in infancy), I was spoiled. I used to tell my brothers that they spoiled me until I was about five, then they beat the crap out of me, because they couldn't stand the spoiled brat they had created.

I was born with platinum blonde curly hair which began darkening by age five and kept on getting darker until it was very dark brown, just in time for it to turn gray. My brother Dean and I had blue eyes while every other person in our big family had brown eyes. I think I was a bratty kid. I must have been, because I remember getting quite a few switchings with a stick off the peach tree. Of course, that was in the day when spankings were still fashionable and before it became child abuse.

Just after my thirteenth birthday Mom died. My happy-go-lucky world came to a halt that year. I lost the person closest to me in the whole world, and I grew up fast. I did not have life figured out after all. Life was not a bowl of corn flakes. I never really got over her dying, but I did get through it. Some days, even now, I still see her face and hear her words as if she were sitting across from me, and it has been fifty-five years since she died. Our mother/daughter bond was like a strong gold cord binding us forever.

I wanted to be a nurse from an early age. When Mom became sick at home with cancer, I became more sold on nursing as a career, even though my interest tests showed I should be a social worker or teacher. Mom's caregivers gave me little jobs to do like boiling the hypodermic needles and syringes. The nurse showed me how to give shots to an orange, in case I ever needed to give Mom a shot ... I actually gave her a shot one night when she was in terrible pain and the nurse was not available. Dr. Buchanan walked me through it by phone.

A good student and a popular kid, I didn't give my dad many problems in high school, although I was mouthy. For some reason I felt mad at him because Mom died. I did not realize why I was mad at him until years later.

I knew that we did not have money for me to go away to school, and yet I had such a hankering to be a nurse. My best friend Mary Frances also wanted to be a nurse. We used to daydream about being a nurse in a big hospital. We also day-dreamed about getting married and having babies. We both wanted children.

I told her, "When I have my first girl, I am going to name her Mary Frances, after you."

How would I ever get the money to go to nursing school? I wondered. I used to daydream that I would perform a heroic measure like pulling someone from a burning house, and I would be rewarded with twenty thousand dollars. Then, I could go to school.

You noticed that I did not say we were poor? To me there was a big difference between lacking money and being poor. We always had plenty of delicious food to eat. Living on the edge of town we were able to have a cow, a pig, chickens, and a couple ducks (which my brother Leo and I named Tom and Jerry). We also had a huge garden. In those days we never saw a slice of store-bought bread in our house. I used to beg Mom to buy a loaf of "real" bread from the store. With homemade bread and cinnamon rolls to eat, some of my friends said that we ate better than they did. No, we were not poor. We always knew we were loved too. *Why didn't my Mary feel loved as I did? Why weren't we as close as my mom and me? That was my dream.*

In our home laughing, fighting, crying, and hugs were plentiful. You could say that we "let it all hang out." We all worked hard. I had a paper route at age twelve and baby-sat for a quarter an hour at every opportunity. In eighth grade I had a small job typing cards on Saturday mornings at the Wray hospital. As soon as I was sixteen, Bertha Utz, the superintendent of the hospital, gave me a job as a nurses' aide. Mrs. Utz knew I wanted to be a nurse and let me rub elbows with the nurses, I'm sure to encourage me toward being a nurse. Some people thought she was stern. I had a huge respect for her and found her to be quite kind.

Mom made all my clothes. I would choose my clothes out of the Sears catalog, and then Mom would make a pattern out of newspaper, and sew them for me. When I was real little, she made them from printed flour sacks, which we bought by hundred pound bags. We would go to Fred's grocery, where I would choose the print I liked, and then Mom would purchase that bag of flour. I could not wait until she used up all the flour so she could sew my dress. She also remodeled hand-me-downs which I thought were quite nice. Mom took me to the Wray Christian Church every Sunday. In high school I sang in the church choir.

One thing for sure, Mom never worked outside the home a day in her life. *Could that be the problem with Mary? Because I was working, did she think I was not there for her? Was it diluting my attention toward her?*

I liked being a tomboy and thought I was just as tough as any of the boys at school or home. Mom scolded me about my bruises and torn clothes and begged me to act like a lady. I took pride in being tough. I especially liked football. I'm not sure what the other girls did during recess, but I played tackle football with the boys. I was not even afraid to tackle Larry Renzelman, who was our biggest football player. When we were freshmen in high school, some of the boys went to Coach Eastin and asked him if I could play freshman football. Since I baby sat for Coach Eastin, he knew me pretty well. He came to me and said, "Gayle Muree, you are not going to play football. You are a girl and it is time you started acting like one!" I respected Coach Eastin and his wife Evie, so I became a football *fan*, and I tried very hard to act like a girl. I had to stay tough though, because I had to hold my own with my seven brothers.

While a senior in high school, I heard about a school loan I might be able to get from the Wray Woman's Club so I could go to nurses' training. I applied for it and received it. My dad was upset. He felt that taking a loan to go to school was accepting charity. He said, "Why do you want to go on to school, anyway? You already work as a nurses' aide at the hospital. Isn't that good enough? No one in our family has ever taken charity." You could easily see my dad was not high on education … though he wasn't short on pride. Dad had finished eighth grade and Mom only sixth grade. I could never figure out how my dad became such a math whiz and Mom such a good speller and reader. I guess they taught themselves.

It pretty much took a town project to get me off to school. Nell Bullard sewed me a sharp looking dress of red paisley cotton. Bertha Utz made a laundry bag and a sewing kit for me. Mrs. Wells, my old Sunday school teacher, gave me some beautiful embroidered pillow slips. My married sister Joan saw that I had everything else I needed. You could say that I went to nurses' training by the seat of my pants and in spite of a lack of money.

When I arrived in Denver, I found that St. Lukes had doubled their tuition. I had been using a two-year old booklet and didn't know about the new rates.

Guess that's what happened when a kid tried to go away to school on their own steam. I shed tears as I went to the Director's office to tell her that I did not have enough money to stay. Ms. DeYoung was gentle and even finagled another loan for me from the Denver Lion's Club. I stayed in Denver after all. I wanted to be a nurse more than anything. Not just any nurse. I wanted to be like Bertha Utz and Grace Cope, my favorite nurses at the Wray Hospital.

And so I began my nurses' training. My best friend Mary Frances Staples and her family had moved to Seattle after our senior year of high school, and Mary began nurses' training at St. Cabrini Hospital in Seattle. At the end of my first quarter at St. Lukes, Mary's dad suffered a heart attack at the wheel of his car and died in Seattle. He was 45 years old, and it happened the day after Christmas. They were devastated and I was too.

Mary asked me to come there and be with them. She said I could finish nursing school in Seattle with her. Since I had lost my mom, I knew what they were going through. I felt like I was part of their family and I wanted to be there with them. Besides losing their breadwinner, none of them knew how to drive a car.

I had become part of the Staples family after Mom died. My father was often working out of town, so I would have been alone much of the time if not for the Staples family. Mary's mom, Fern, said to me, "Gayle, if you and Mary are going to be friends, you will have to go by our rules." I readily agreed. I even minded their rules when I was away from them. If Mary had to be in by 10:30, then I would also be in by 10:30. I felt comforted that I too had rules. The Staples family included me in everything, even vacations.

I felt a strong urge to go to Seattle to be with them. In those days it was practically impossible to transfer between nursing schools, since each curriculum was different. Between Mary and me and both schools working together, the transfer was accomplished. I was able to take my credits and go to Seattle to be with my second family. I had never been out of Colorado, and now I was headed for Seattle, half the country away. I would soon learn the meaning of homesickness.

I did well in nurses' training and was awarded the Scholarship/Leadership Award as a senior and was elected president of the student body. Mary and I were inseparable. I always felt like Mary was my sister. We could and did share everything with each other. Mary had a hard time dealing with her dad's death. The whole class tried to bring her through her grief, but I think it stayed with her for years.

In my third year of training, I met my future husband Raul who was a General Practice resident at our hospital. Raul was Filipino and was training in the states on an exchange visitor visa. Raul and I were married two days after I was graduated from nurses' training. Mary Frances was married the same day we were grad-uated.

Foreign medical graduates could not practice in the U.S. until they passed the ECFMG, an exam for foreign medical graduates. Only then could they take the board exams in any state in the U.S. Before passing the exam Raul could only assist in surgery and do histories and physicals. He did that while I worked at Cabrini Hospital ... between babies, that is. Steve was born in 1961, Matt in 1962, and Mike in 1963. Boom, boom, boom. All were C-Sections.

In 1964 Raul and I and our three little boys moved to Tucson, Arizona, where Raul began a four-year surgical residency. I became pregnant with our fourth child Bruce during Raul's second year of residency. Steve was now 5, Matt 4, and Mike 3. I was facing my fourth Caesarean section, which our physician said would have to be our last. I wanted a daughter, but since this had been a troubled pregnancy, I only hoped and prayed that the baby, whatever the sex, would be healthy.

I was pretty sure I would have another boy and mentioned this to Raul. He said to me, "Don't worry, Gayle, if we have another boy, we'll adopt a baby girl later." I was satisfied.

Our healthy boy Bruce joined our family in August and I was elated. When Bruce was six months old, Raul changed his mind about adopting a girl. (Not because of Bruce!) "Gayle, we have enough kids, look how busy we are ... we can't adopt another child."

"But you said ..." I whined.

"I know what I said, but I've changed my mind. How could we handle another one?" he raised his voice. I did not say anymore. I didn't bring it up again, but my heart never parted with the hope of having a daughter. I tearfully proceeded to give away all the baby paraphernalia as soon as we no longer needed it.

While living in Tucson I worked as a nurse in the recovery room at a local hospital. Since finding good baby-sitters was always a challenge, a co-worker sug-gested that we take in unwed mothers who would stay with us until their babies were born. We would pay them so they could pay for the birth and in return they would baby-sit and help around the house. That was the beginning of our taking in unwed mothers.

I quit work after Bruce's birth, but the agency still wanted us to take in the unwed mothers. Some of these mothers were giving up their baby for adoption, and some were going to keep them. I went to the hospital with them and helped them through labor and delivery. If they kept the baby, I did my best to teach them how to be a mother. If they gave the baby up, I comforted them. We also had two other teen-age foster children during that time. All together we had twenty different foster children/unwed mothers during our four years in Tucson.

Raul passed his ECFMG exam and then began to study for state boards. In July of 1968 we moved to Larned, Kansas, where Raul became the Medical Director of the fifty-bed medical infirmary at Larned State Hospital (a mental hospital). This was an interim position to allow Raul more time to study. Our goal was to live in Larned until Raul passed his Wisconsin State Boards. Then we would join our friends Don and Peg in Fort Atkinson, Wisconsin, where Don was already in a group practice.

Larned was a farm community with a population of 5,000. The state hospital was the biggest employer. A short time after we were settled, Raul came home one evening and shocked me, "Gayle, if you still want to adopt a baby girl, let's do it!"

That was out of the clear blue. What could have prompted him to come to this conclusion? "Do you know what you're saying?" I asked.

"I don't think you'll be happy until you have a daughter. I'd like a girl too. I don't know how we'll manage the money, but I guess we'll be okay," he said.

"Raul, don't say it unless you mean it. Don't come home tomorrow and say you've changed your mind. I think you know what this means to me."

"I'm serious."

I didn't ask any more questions for fear he would change his mind. "I'm sure the money will work out." I told him." *Maybe I will have a baby named Mary Frances after all.* I could not stop smiling.

I wasted no time in setting an appointment with Catholic Social Services. Within one week we had a visit from Father John, a handsome priest, who was a social worker at Catholic Charities in Great Bend, Kansas. He was about our age and we liked his sense of humor and down-to-earth manner.

"Father, we have four healthy active boys and now our wish is to have a girl. We would like a mixed racial child, because we are a mixed racial family. We would also consider a handicapped child or an older child. We do not want to take an infant for whom a childless couple is waiting." We had several sessions with Father John and were approved. The week after we were approved to get a baby, Raul received a huge raise. The state job which Raul had been doing had been reclassified to a much higher level.

"Gayle, you have a sixth sense. You said the money would work out," Raul smiled and shook his head as if he could not believe me.

Three months later Father John called, "We have a new baby of Mexican-American heritage, born in Wichita … think you two would like to consider her?"

"Are you kidding?" I could barely breathe. It had only been three months since we were approved. "I must call Raul at work and then I will call you back." My hands shook as I called Raul.

"Guess what?" I said, "They have our baby girl in Wichita and want to know if we want her. She is Mexican-American."

"What do we know about the mother and father?" he asked.

"We know the mother was sixteen and extremely rebellious. We don't know who the father was." I said. "Does it matter to you?" I asked. He never answered. Maybe I didn't give him a chance.

"Raul, I want her. I know she is meant for us." I could barely get the words out. I tried not to sound too desperate.

"Then let's say we'll consider her," he said. The arrangements were made. On Thursday of the following week Father John piloted a plane to Wichita, where he picked up our new daughter from the hospital. He brought along a student nurse who cared for the baby on the trip back to Great Bend, Kansas. We met them at the hospital.

You might wonder why a person with four healthy boys would want so badly to have a daughter. When my mom died I received a lifetime legacy of love from our closeness, and I wanted to repeat that with my own daughter. I loved our four boys and felt very close to them, but I also felt they would benefit from having a girl in the family. I also liked the idea of having a big family. I felt close to my seven living brothers and my sister, and we had such a fun time growing up. Even now when we all came together it was great fun.

When Raul first met my family, my big brothers all hugged him, much to his surprise. Raul actually blushed. It did not take him long before he could hug with the best of them. Being part of a big family was a new experience for Raul, as he only had one sister.

By the time of the adoption our boys were Steven, age seven, Matt age six, Mike age five, and Bruce age two. Those healthy, active, bright little guys were thrilled at the thought of having a baby sister. That is, except Bruce, who wanted a baby brother. "No girls!" he would say with his index finger poking at us and a scowl on his face like a stern parent. The combination of Filipino and blue-eyed Caucasian, produced boys with beautiful coloring. They were handsome and received lots of attention wherever we took them. I marveled at how much they looked alike and yet how they were such individuals.

Steve was very much the big brother and Mama's helper. He had great patience with his siblings and was a born teacher. Matt, smart, mischievous, assertive and funny, was not sure whether he wanted to follow in his big brother's footsteps or to strike out on his own. Mike was the mellow one, loved everyone and rarely became upset. Bruce was a cute little guy and very independent. At age two Bruce did not like to wear clothes. I often received a calls from my neighbor, "Bruce took off his clothes again and is running down the sidewalk without a stitch."

We only had a few days to get ready for our new daughter Mary Frances, who was named after my best friend, just like I promised her when we were in high school. The Great Bend hospital was ten miles from Larned. My friend Grethe helped us get ready and would watch the boys while we went to fetch our new baby girl. Grethe had two adopted children, Damien and Heidi. It was a new experience expecting a baby without having a big tummy, and without having a cesarean incision. I was perched on top of the world. This time *I* paced the floor and smoked cigarettes along with Raul.

4

Baby Mary

We greeted a grinning Father John, who was holding a tiny bundle when we met him in a private lounge at the Great Bend hospital. In his arms was eight-day-old Mary Frances. Father John handed her to me. What a beautiful baby with lots of dark hair that waved close to her head like a cap. She was sucking her thumb with her four fingers fanned out across her face. She had a dimple in her chin. She opened her eyes and peeked at us through her fingers, as if to say, "Here I am, ready or not."

My husband Raul took one look at her and said, "She is *our* baby. She looks just like our boys did when they were born."

I laughed with tears running down my face. "She is perfect," I said over and over. I could not believe our good fortune at being able to adopt, adding a daughter to our family of four boys.

Father John said, "Shall I take your response as a 'yes' that you want to keep her?"

"Yes," we said at the same time. As I examined our baby to make sure she had all her fingers and toes, visions of ballet lessons and pink tutus danced in my head. A perfect beginning, I thought.

Our arrival home with Mary Frances was chaotic. The boys argued over who would hold her first, who would hold the bottle to feed her, and believe it or not they even wanted to change her diaper, except for the messy ones.

Quite puzzled by the fact that she did not come with plumbing like his, Bruce asked repeatedly, "Why doesn't she have a dingy, Mama? Daddy has one, Stevie has one, Matt has one, Mike has one, Bruce has one; poor Mary does not have one." he would tell us as he projected his sad look.

"She is like Mama, she's a girl." I told him. Already I could see the advantage of adding a girl to our family.

On Mary's first night at home we fed her a bottle at 10:00 P.M. I was expecting her to wake up in three to four hours. When I awoke at 6:00 A.M. she was still sleeping. I panicked. Surely she must be dead. I leaped over to the crib and picked her up. Startled, she began to cry. "Thank God you are okay. Mama thought something was wrong." I told her. Since I was a nurse and mother of four, I knew that sleeping for this long of a period was unusual for an eight-day-old baby. Even Raul as a physician was puzzled. Newborns are usually hungry every three to four hours, and sometimes fuss off and on all night, like our boys did. I remember wondering at the time if something might be wrong with her. But then Raul and I decided that God had decided to reward us with an extra good baby. From then on until she was six weeks old, I set my alarm and gave her a bottle every four hours. Sleep was her favorite thing to do.

The second night of her homecoming I set my alarm for 2:00 A.M. I went into the kitchen to heat her bottle. When I came out, there were our four little boys sitting in a line on the couch, eagerly waiting to feed their baby sister. Each one fed her a little and each one burped her. Bruce, just over two years old, needed a little help here and there, but would not be outdone by his older brothers. I said to Baby Mary Frances, "Honey, you don't know how blessed you are to have these four big brothers to look out for you."

One afternoon when Mary was two weeks old we heard Mike, our third boy who was five, coming down the hall from Mary's room. "Look Mom, how good I'm holding her!" I almost had a heart attack. Mike was carrying Mary ever so carefully, head supported and everything, walking slowly toward us. I did not want to frighten him or hurt his feelings, so I walked slowly toward him and cautiously supported him to the sofa with Mary.

"Honey, until she is older, only a big person like Mama or Daddy can get her out of the crib. When she is able to stand in the crib, you will be able to get her out. By the way, how *did* you get her out of the crib?" I ventured.

"I was very careful, Mama," he said as he rolled his big brown eyes. To this day we have no idea how that five year old plucked that two-week-old baby out of a full-sized crib without hurting her. Angels, maybe.

Mary became prettier every day. She looked so much like her brothers that people found it hard to believe she was adopted. Her dark curly hair framed her face and her big brown eyes twinkled when she smiled. That dimple in her chin was like an exclamation point for her pretty face.

At six weeks old, I stopped waking Mary to feed her. Then she would sleep from 8:00 P.M. to 8:00 A.M. We bragged to our friends about what an exceptionally good baby we had, sleeping twelve hours every night. Mary was also a good eater and when she began eating solid foods she would savor them by moaning "mmm" with each bite.

"She's no fun. She always sleeps. When will she start playing with me?" Bruce complained.

I would often dress Mary in frilly dresses with ruffled bonnets, and Bruce and I would take her for walks in the stroller to show her off to the residents of Larned. She was a fun baby and so good-natured. When our boys were born, they would demand loudly to be fed and changed. Sleeping to them meant cat naps in between rigorous crying, laughing or eating. Mary cried very little, and then it was more like fussing ... not bellowing.

Were girls this different? She was very verbal, cooing and laughing out loud at two months. It was eight months before I came down off my cloud. My joy at having a daughter took my breath away. I dreamed of shopping for prom dresses and of having long personal talks with my daughter. I knew we were going to be close. Raul seemed to be as thrilled as I was. This was, without a doubt, the happiest year of our marriage.

The only negatives I remember: Raul was lukewarm in our bedroom ... he never seemed to want to be intimate with me. This was something that began shortly after we were married and it was not getting any better. I charged it up to the fact that he was extremely busy and dead tired every night. I was tired too, so it was not a big issue.

While we lived in Larned, Raul's parents came from the Philippines for a three-month visit. Prior to their visit, Raul told me, "Adoption is not common in the Philippines, and I don't know if my parents will accept Mary as their own grandchild." I worried that our little girl would not be loved by them. We need not have worried. They made a big to-do over her and carried her around all day. Mother and Father Lagman set about spoiling little Mary Frances.

Raul had not seen his parents in eleven years and it was obvious to me that both parties had changed during that time. Raul wanted Mother to cook Filipino food and his parents wanted to try American food, such as hot dogs and potato salad (which Raul still refused to eat). They said they liked American food, while Raul who had been in the states for eleven years, did not like it. Once in awhile Raul would take me to a drive-in restaurant to have a hamburger. He would not eat anything, but would sit there and giggle, saying, "Look at those crazy Americans chomping on hamburgers as if it were their last meal on earth."

Mother chided Raul about his lack of acceptance of American food. "Shame on you," she would say.

Raul's mother had been a nurse and midwife in the Philippines and was very proud of her son, the doctor. She was full of medical questions and questions about what it was like to be a doctor in the U.S. I could see her eyes twinkling as he related answers to her. She did not, however, appreciate his frequent questioning of her and Father, "Did you wash your hands?" Raul treated our home as if it were the operating room at the hospital … everything was either clean or dirty, and there was no in-between.

Our first baby Steve once played in the toilet, and Raul washed him with surgical soap. When Steve was learning to crawl, Raul placed a wall to wall blanket on top of our carpet so Steve could crawl on it. He spent lots of time retrieving Steve as he crawled off the blanket. I laughed and teased him about it. I told him when I was a kid, I made mud-pies and ate them. He shook his head in disbelief.

Mary had a way of making fussing sounds before she went to sleep, and Mother would quickly retrieve her, saying "She is not ready to sleep."

Finally, I had to tell her, "Mother, Mary likes to fuss a little on her way to sleeping. She's not crying. It's just her way of going to sleep." Mother finally agreed to it, but I knew I had hurt her feelings. They were kind and sensitive people.

The grandparent visit was sometimes difficult. They did not understand many of our ways … especially discipline of the children. They seemed to think it was mean to make the boys sit on a chair or to give them a swat.

Bruce was a mischievous little guy and a climber. One day Mother and Father were watching two-year-old Bruce while I showered. When I came out, I found Bruce on top of our highest kitchen cupboard, near the ceiling. Mother and Father were sitting on the couch watching him saying, "No, no, Brucie," in their soft little voices. No emergency to them. I had to get the ladder to retrieve him, and I gave him a big swat.

Mother said, "I can't bear to see him hurt."

"Mother, he is not hurt at all, but he could have been, if he fell!" I said firmly. "You should have called me. He could have been seriously injured." Those were the days when it was still okay (even expected) to spank your child. I suppose by today's standards I would have been considered a child abuser. Often, when Raul arrived home, Mother and Father would take him into the bedroom and they would speak their native tongue Tagalog for awhile. I imagined they were telling him all kinds of bad things about me, because every once in awhile I would hear them say, "Gayle." Raul denied that they were talking about me, but I could tell the way he was grinning that he wasn't about to be caught in the middle of that.

Mother and Father Lagman had expected instant love and affection from the boys. The boys remained somewhat distant from them … a little afraid of them, it seemed. I tried to get Mother and Father to play with the boys, so they could develop a closeness … but Mother and Father felt the closeness should be automatic. Perhaps that was a cultural gap. Instead, they showered all their affection on baby Mary who ate it up.

Raul was studying in earnest for his board exams. In preparation, I would quiz him late into the night with review questions. Raul did not have much confidence in himself. He kept saying, "I don't think I can pass this exam. I will probably have to take the exam two or three times." I don't know why he felt that way because he had received one of the highest scores on his medical boards when he took them in the Philippines. Raul never seemed to have a very high opinion of himself.

After Mother and Father returned to the Philippines, Raul flew to Wisconsin to take his boards, which he passed on his first attempt. We began making plans to move to Fort Atkinson, Wisconsin. I was reluctant to leave this little town where we had been so happy. Dr. Brenner, the local physician, invited Raul to stay and practice with him. We considered it, but in the end decided to stick with our plan. I have often wondered how our lives would have unfolded, had we stayed in Larned.

5

And Then There Were Six

In Fort Atkinson we bought a big, barn-like seventy-five-year-old home, one block from the Rock River, on a street with other big old homes and lots of shade trees. To me it looked like Pleasant Street, USA. The kids ran all over the neighborhood making friends with the other children. Don and Peg, the friends we had made in Tucson, introduced us to others and took us out dancing and dining with them. Their five children and our five spent much time together.

If you were to ask me at that time if I had a good marriage I would have said "Absolutely." There were times that I squelched feelings of jealousy when Raul flirted with other women. I decided that most men behaved that way. I read somewhere that it doesn't matter where the man gets his appetite, as long as he comes home to dine. The truth was that Raul did not seem attracted to me in a sexual sense. I did not want to admit it; however, I was always the instigator when it came to lovemaking. He was nice to me and seemed to care about me ... like one cares about his mother. I tried to talk to him about it. "Why don't you want to be intimate with me? We *are* man and wife."

He always had an excuse. "I have surgery tomorrow and I need to be sharp," he would often say. Or, "I've had a hard day and I'm tired," or, "I have a headache." I always heard it was women who frequently professed to have headaches. Sometimes he told me that I was oversexed, whatever that meant in a marriage. I blamed myself for not being attractive enough. I tried to spruce myself up a bit, but it didn't accomplish anything; then I would become even more disappointed.

Mary was becoming a very spoiled eighteen-month-old, so Raul and I decided that we should adopt another girl to complete our family. We had a family meeting and agreed that we would apply to a program in Wisconsin for hard-to-place children. "Children Who Wait" was an interagency program designed to place older children, mixed racial, handicapped, etc. We were blessed to have five healthy children; now we would ask for a child who may have some special needs.

Since we were a licensed foster home we were asked to take in newborns who were awaiting adoption. We were told that we would probably have them about two weeks before they were adopted. Our first placement was a cute little bundle with *red* hair, which was quite a novelty in our family. We called her Sarah Jane. We had Sarah for six weeks because she was showing signs of allergy that had to be checked out before the agency would release her. Of course, we fell in love with her. It was a sad day when she left us to go to her permanent home. We would have tried to adopt her ourselves, but at that time there was a rule that you could not adopt foster children in your care ... such a dumb rule.

We all agreed that the first child the agency came up with was meant to be ours. After going through all the red tape, we were approved. Our social worker, Mrs. Olson from LaCrosse, Wisconsin, was passing through town one day and stopped in to pay a friendly visit. "Did you find a baby for us?" I asked.

"No," she said, "I was just passing through and thought I would say hello." The only child I have right now is a little girl who is almost two, but she's not ready for adoption yet because of some health problems. I do happen to have a photo of her." She pulled out a snapshot of a tiny two-year-old girl with a pixie haircut and a big smile.

"That's our baby!" shouted oldest son Steve. "Remember, Mom, the first one they come up with is ours. That's what we said!"

"You're right, honey. We'll have to talk to Daddy and see what he says." I asked Mrs. Olson, "Is it even possible for us to adopt her?"

She said, "I will have to check with the doctors and see when they plan to release her. She is the child of a drug user and was born with multiple anomalies. They are checking out all those things right now."

"What kinds of things?" I asked.

"First off, she was three pounds at full term birth. The doctors say she has congenital smallness. She has tight hips which causes her legs to spread only 45 degrees, her nose was wrong side out at birth, she has a left torticollis, where the muscles in one side of her face are pulled down into her neck, making one side of her face flat and the other side rounded. She was born with club feet which are now corrected. Her cranial soft spots were closed at birth; therefore, the doctors are classifying her as a microcephalic (small head which may not be able to handle expansion of the brain). Most of the doctors say she is mentally handicapped, although one of the psychologists feels that she has normal intelligence, because on some of her tests she did very well, which one would not expect with a mentally challenged child. It was his thought that she may not have had enough stimulation to learn properly. He also felt that her social and emotional immaturity may have caused her to do poorly on the tests they had administered." She paused. "And that is the story of little Kim." Mrs. Olson looked over at us; I think to gauge our reactions.

"Wow, all of that for one tiny girl?" I felt overcome with compassion for this tiny girl whom I had yet to meet.

"That's what happens when drug users take drugs during pregnancy," Mrs. Olson said.

The following week Mrs. Olson got the go-ahead from the doctors, and Raul and I made the trip to LaCrosse to meet almost two-year-old, tiny Kim. We were placed into a room where Kim was playing with some blocks at a small table. She mostly ignored us, although occasionally she glanced our way. We spoke to her quietly, complimenting her on building towers with the blocks. This went on for fifteen minutes or so. Then one of the towers collapsed and some of the blocks fell off the table. I pretended to jump and looked startled. She laughed and cackled in a very deep voice. She repeated this over and over knocking a block on the floor and enjoying my reaction. We stayed about an hour. Kim let me hold her before we parted, but kept her body stiff, not yet trusting closeness. She was so tiny at two years old; it was like holding a doll. She waved good-bye to us. She already had my heart.

We visited with Mrs. Olson. She explained, "With older children it is usually better to place the child gradually. Also, you should know that bonding with an older child usually takes longer than with an infant. If you are interested in carrying this further, we would begin with home visits." Raul and I agreed that we wanted to go ahead with plans to adopt Kim if the home visits went well.

Raul and I discussed this all the way home. Raul said, "I know Mary is spoiled and needs a sister, but I am worried about making Mary feel displaced."

"Raul, we have been through this with the boys. There is always a period of adjustment when the new kid comes along. I think it's good for them in the long run. Mary will be jealous, and she will get over it," I assured him.

The next week Mrs. Olson and her helper brought Kim for a visit. She explained, "If you decide to go ahead with the adoption, you may change her name if you want." She had been called Kim for two years, and I worried that it may confuse her if we changed it. Mrs. Olson and her helper dropped Kim off on a Tuesday morning and said they would return around four p.m.

Kim was shy at first, but seemed to remember me. She followed Mary around right away and tried to copy everything Mary did. Kim did not talk, except to say "Boo," the name she gave to a cloth diaper that she carried around like a security blanket. When she wanted something, she grunted and pointed. "Uh, uh." The boys came home at noon for lunch to see their candidate for a new sister. They played with her and had her laughing right away. She rewarded them frequently with that deep voice cackle of hers. She seemed delighted to have playmates. The boys objected to going back to school for the afternoon. I assured them that Kim would still be there when they returned. "We want to keep her, Mom," they said as they went out the door.

I watched as Mary sized up Kim. We also had a new St. Bernard puppy, Samantha (Sam for short), who got into the act. Kim was afraid of Sam at first, but they quickly made friends. Mary was showing Kim all of her toys and abilities. She would climb up on the counter and then watch as Kim struggled to follow her. She would show Kim her toys, but did not want Kim to play with any of them. I could see that sharing was going to be a challenge ... one that I would expect to have.

When Mrs. Olson came back to get Kim, the boys were home from school and were actively playing with Kim and Mary. Kim paid no attention to Mrs. Olson. Raul had come home from work early. After about an hour of observing, Mrs. Olson said, "Dr. and Mrs. Lagman, how do you feel this is going?

I answered for both of us. "I think Kim is definitely our little girl.

She is doing well here."

"What would you say if we decided to extend Kim's visit here and leave her for a week with you? She seems to fit in so well. We think it would be in her best interest not to take her back and forth and confuse her. If it goes well this week we will bring all her things next week. What do you think? I will call you during the week to see how it's going."

"We would like that." I said. Raul didn't say much, but seemed pleased at how Kim was relating to our other kids. I said, "This is meant to be. All the pieces are falling into place, just like with Mary's adoption." And now we were six ... four boys and two girls. Our family was complete.

We were told that Kim had a very low frustration level and was used to being held much of the time by the foster parents. With six children and a St. Bernard, I knew Kim was not going to be held much of the time! Those first few weeks were tough. She always wanted to be held, the dog wanted to be walked, Mary was becoming jealous. When I could not hold Kim she would cry hysterically, the kind of cry I would expect if she had broken a bone.

The boys tried to hold her when they were around, but I told them, "Kim has to learn how to entertain herself, and you could help by teaching her how to play. Also, don't give in to her grunting and pointing when she wants something, unless she makes some effort to say it. Repeat the word over and over to her." All day long I could hear them say, "Say 'water' or "say 'milk,'" on and on like little teachers.

Mary was not so gracious. She would cover her ears and tell us, "She cries too loud! Make her stop!"

Three weeks after Kim joined our family, all of the children were seated around the big dining room table. Each one had their breakfast except Kim. I kept saying from the kitchen, "Tell Mama what you want for breakfast, Kim." Kim would just beat on her bowl with her spoon and yell loudly.

After repeating my "what do you want for breakfast" phrase a half dozen times, I heard this deep voice shout, "I want an egg!" Kim not only said a word, she said an entire sentence!

The boys picked her up and danced around with her. Mary was giggling. "She talked! She talked! Kim can talk!" Kim was laughing and looking very proud of herself. From that time on she chattered continuously. It was as if the language had been dammed up inside her and the dam finally broke.

And so began the separate and yet connected stories of our two adopted daughters. Kim had her story and Mary had her story. Little did we know that *both* our little girls' lives were going to be complicated because of biological mothers who chose to use drugs during their pregnancies. We were soon to find out that parenting these two little females would not be easy. Each daughter brought with them a unique set of challenges. This is Mary's story. She was the squeaky wheel, the one who demanded the oil.

Our first summer in Fort, my dad Gail, my stepmother Gladys, my brother Bud, and my sister-in-law Irma, paid us a visit in Fort Atkinson. We were sitting out back at the picnic table having a cocktail. Bud had made himself Scotch-on-the-Rocks, when a friend drove up out front to bring us some fishing poles. We all went out front, leaving our drinks on the table. When we came back, Bud said, "I would have sworn I poured myself a Scotch, but my glass is empty."

We all teased him, "Perhaps you've had enough already."

About half an hour later we were inside when I saw Mary through our glass front door, staggering up the front steps. I ran out and grabbed her to keep her from falling. She smelled like a distillery and she acted drunk. She was slurring her speech and her eyes seemed unable to focus. We then realized where Bud's Scotch went. We were astounded that Mary could have drunk a glass of straight Scotch. Most little ones would turn their nose up at even a smell of hard liquor. She had downed that Scotch in the few minutes that it took us to go out front and get the fishing poles.

Had Raul not been a physician, we would have had to take her to the E.R. As it was we had to keep her awake and Raul gave her a shot of Sparine, like they gave to alcoholics. She threw up and got rid of some of it. We watched her all night for alcohol toxicity. This was our first inkling that Mary might have been born a fetal alcohol baby ... a born alcoholic. We then recalled how much she slept at eight days old when she first came home with us. *Was this possible?* We watched her closely after that and removed any access to alcohol.

It was a wild winter. Our St. Bernard Sam had hip problems. The Vet said I had to walk her mile a day, but actually she walked me. One night at dinner I had placed the roast by Raul to carve, and we were all involved in talking about the events of the day. When Raul picked up the knife to carve the roast, it was gone! The platter was empty. We looked around for Sam. There she was sitting in the living room licking her chops. Raul said in a very loud voice, "Either that dog goes or I go!" He left the table, obviously upset. We had much going on at our house. I thought about how I could reduce the craziness and the next day I began looking for a good home for Sam. We gave her to our egg man who lived on a farm.

I never seemed to be able to keep the house as neat as Raul wanted. He would come home each evening and ask, "What did you do all day?" It irritated me, especially after I had run all day. We had not lived in Fort very long, when I read a Family Circus cartoon in the Sunday paper. In the cartoon their house was a mess, kids were in their pajamas, mother was still in her nightgown. Dishes were everywhere. The father comes in the door with his brief case looking shocked at the mess. The mother says to him, "You always asked what I did all day ... well, today I didn't do it."

I made up my mind that we would perform that cartoon for Raul. I chose a day the kids were off from school. I told them, "Today we are not going to do any work. We are not even going to get dressed. We are just going to play all day!" They jumped up and down. All day they kept looking at me to see if I would change my mind. Even little Mary and Kim were having a ball. I didn't make them pick up their toys or take their dishes to the kitchen. What a mess we were creating, which ultimately we would have to clean ... but right then we were having fun. Even *I* did not realize how much I did in one day.

All was going well until the doorbell rang about 4:00 P.M. We could not hide because we had an oval, beveled glass front door. There stood a woman with a plate of cookies. Can you imagine? I had not combed my hair. The place was a shambles. We were still in our pajamas. I sheepishly opened the door and she said, "Hi, I am your neighbor, Odette. I just came by to welcome you and say hello." She was so calm; she did not even look amazed by the mess she could easily see.

"Do you have a good sense of humor?" I asked.

"I think so," she answered with a smile.

"Well, then come on in and we'll have a cup of coffee while I explain this mess to you." I told her what we were doing and showed her the Family Circus cartoon. She laughed. We became good friends. She had seven kids, so I doubt if I shocked her too much.

When Raul arrived home, he seemed unable to take it all in. "What's going on? Are you sick? Why are things such a mess?"

Now the words I had been dying to say, "Remember how you always ask me what I did all day? Well, today I didn't do it!" He didn't seem to think it was funny and just shook his head, as if to say that I was a hopeless case. More importantly, he never again asked me, "What did you do all day?"

The kids would often say to me, "Mom, remember that day when we played all day, can we do it again?" While Moms and Dads appreciate a clean and orderly house, kids seem to know what is really important.

The bright spot of that winter was Katherine. She was a woman in her seventies, but looked sixty. She came to clean our house once a week and became our baby sitter. When she came into our house, a sort of calm surrounded us. She was much like my mother and I enjoyed having coffee and visiting with her. She became my friend. This arrangement gave me a day off once a week, which I desperately needed. I could then relax because I knew the kids were in good hands. I would get my hair done and have lunch with Myrtie, my friend Peg's mom. Myrtie always had a good joke for me and would send "good pills" home for the kids. They were little tubes of candy wrapped in cellophane. She would tell the kids that eating those good pills would make them be good. Hopefully, they would believe it and act accordingly. After my outing I would go home to a clean house and happy kids. Katherine was our Mary Poppins.

It was about this time that we had a call from Social Services. They were looking to place an unwed mother to stay in a private home until her baby was born, which she would be giving up for adoption. Social Service indicated that she was nineteen and could be a good mother's helper with the kids. Since we had helped so many of them through their pregnancy and delivery in Tucson, it seemed like a no-brainer to do it again.

6

Clouds on the Horizon

Jill came to stay with us. She was six months pregnant. She was a pretty, nine-teen-year-old girl who read her Bible out loud every day and night and then would hang her sexy underwear everywhere to dry, especially where Raul would see it or have to walk through it. I asked her kindly not to do it. She flirted with Raul. I suspected she suffered from "doctor awe." Jill seemed to think that Raul was some kind of god. He seemed flattered and amused by it, I could tell. I felt uncomfortable with what I saw as a mutual attraction or chemistry between them. I was jealous too. I decided that it would be not be wise to leave them alone. Why, I asked myself, did he seem to be attracted to every woman but me? I didn't think I was unattractive. I knew I was not drop-dead gorgeous. Men in my earlier life seemed to find me attractive, and I had not let myself go downhill.

One night I received a call to substitute at bowling. I would only agree to bowl if Jill would go with me. "Will you go bowling with me tonight?" I asked.

"Sure," she said. So I agreed to sub. When it was time to depart, Jill said, "I'm not feeling well tonight, I think I need to stay home." My heart sank.

"Maybe you just need to get out," I said.

She would not change her mind. I had to go on to the bowling alley, but I felt lousy all evening. *Something sexual is going to happen between Raul and Jill. I feel nauseated. I just feel it in my bones. I am filled with dread. I am also afraid if something does happen between them, I won't find out, and then I will be the fool. Being made the fool bothers me almost as much as the fact that Raul is attracted to another woman.*

I devised a plan as I drove home. I knew that Jill was not the smartest person. I went into the house and found Jill alone in the living room watching TV. "Where is Raul?" I asked.

"He just went to bed," she said, looking as guilty as any person I have ever seen.

"Why did you do it with Raul?" I asked bluntly.

She looked up with her mouth open and said, "How did you know?"

"You just told me," I said. She looked confused. She chattered on and on about how she had wanted Raul (she called him Dr. Lagman) to listen to the baby's heartbeat to make sure it was all right, and … well, things "just got out of hand." She was matter-of-fact about it, as if she were reporting the news on channel four. On the other hand I was not prepared for the whole body shock I felt at her answer. Reality was always more than I wanted. Again.

"Where were the kids while this was going on?" I asked.

"They were in bed asleep," she said, looking away from me.

I left her there and dragged myself up the stairs. I now understood the meaning of a heavy heart. It felt so heavy that it was all I could do to stand upright. I went into the bathroom. I experienced so many conflicting thoughts in my head that it was difficult to sort them out. I felt a chill come over me that I had never experienced before … a deep down bone chill. I may not have been shaking on the outside, but I was shaking violently on the inside. I checked on the kids and gave them all a kiss as they slept. As I looked at them my tears fell. What would happen to all of us now? I finally went to bed. I could tell Raul was not sleeping because he was not snoring. In the dark I sharply whispered to him, "How could you do such a thing?"

"Like what?"

"Have sex with Jill."

He was silent for awhile and then he said, "How did you find out?" The chill went deeper and deeper.

"She told me," I whispered. "You never want to have sex with me, and yet you fall for this little Bible-reading whore!"

"I did not fall for her. It was just one of those things. It doesn't mean anything." he said.

"Bull shit," I offered back. "It may not mean anything to you, but it does to me. Get her out of this house," I said. "Katherine comes tomorrow. I will be leaving. When I get back *she* better be gone. You may be leaving too." I took my pillows and went into the bathroom where I lay in the empty bathtub all night and cried and chilled. In the space of an evening my marriage was in the toilet. We had six kids. What now? What use am I to anyone? I can't even keep a marriage together. I felt betrayed by my husband and by a woman I was trying to help. I felt like I could never function again as a wife and mother. I felt like a pitiful piece of crap, stepped on and ground in.

The next morning I faked cheerfulness for the kids and got them off to school. I did not speak to Raul or to Jill, except to say to her, "You are out of here. Pack up." She was back at reading her Bible again. Maybe she was faking it and really did not know how to read. If she did know how to read, she sure didn't comprehend that part about adultery. She did not say a word to me.

When Katherine arrived I could not look her in the eye. She was so perceptive that I'm sure she knew something was wrong with me. I kissed Bruce and Mary and Kim and told them I would be back later that day. They didn't seem to care … they had Katherine. I could not wait to get into my car and take off. I did not know where I was going. I wanted to get lost. I drove out into the country. I remember thinking that my pain could be over very fast if I were to drive in front of a semi. In my mind the primary thought was *my husband, and the father of our six kids, prefers another woman over me.* After a few hours I realized that it was probably not safe for me to be out driving alone with the kind of thoughts I was having.

I drove to my friend Bev's house where I fell apart. "I don't want to live. My whole world has been turned upside down. I can't function." I cried and talked and Bev listened.

"Gayle, is there anyone in your family that I can call? You need family." I hated to involve my family. I was ashamed that we were having trouble. I finally gave her the name of my brother Dean. She called him. Three of my family members hopped on a plane from Tucson and were there the next day. I must have been on automatic pilot during this period because I don't remember how I took care of the kids or the house. I had the urge to end my life. I felt it was over.

I loved Raul. *How could he do this to me and to our family? It must be my fault. I am not attractive enough.*

My family worked hard to try to keep us together and to get me over the crisis. The only hope I could see for me or for the marriage was counseling. It was hard to stop having thoughts about ending my life. I teetered back and forth from wanting to end my life and then thinking about our children and their angel faces. I finally realized that I could not leave them behind, no matter what. What a hopeless feeling when part of you wants to die and another part says you have to live.

My family persuaded Raul to arrange counseling immediately. I insisted on a psychiatrist because I felt the problems might be deep-seated and complex. We selected Dr. Sparks in Madison, thirty miles away. We were to go every Tuesday on Raul's day off when Katherine would be there to watch the kids.

Our kids seemed to sense that all was not well. Raul and I did not argue. It was if we shared a terrible sadness. Steve took on a strong role as big brother, playing with his younger siblings to keep them occupied. The boys were extra good and did not do their usual rough-housing. Mary and Kim were not in the least demanding. They played well together. They all seemed to sense that we needed space.

And so began a year of marriage counseling. Every week, on our way to Madison, Raul would rehearse me on what I could and what I could *not* tell Dr. Sparks.

Dr. Sparks asked Raul, "Why do you think you are not attracted to Gayle?"

"I'm not sure. When I was a little boy I was thrilled with new toys, but after playing with them a short time, I became bored and would put them on the shelf and I never want to play with them again. I guess that's how I feel about Gayle."

I was no longer the new toy. That sure did not make me feel any better. After a few months of counseling I was fed up. I stood up in our session and said, "I am sick and tired of this. These sessions are like a 'good old boys" club. Raul tells me everything that I can or cannot say, and you two sit there and talk about nothing for a whole hour. You're not getting the true picture of this relationship at all!" I talked and paced the floor. They were both quiet as I spouted truths about how things *really* were. I told them about Raul's escapade with Jill, his attraction to other women, as well as his lack of attraction to me. "How do you expect this doctor to help us if you don't tell him the truth?" I asked Raul.

"I want to see you, Gayle, by yourself for the next few times, and then I will meet with Raul by himself," Dr. Sparks said. "There are lots of feelings here that we need to explore on an individual basis."

I felt hopeful that this might be the beginning of progress. Raul was becoming more communicative and occasionally affectionate. I wondered if he were trying to please me so I would call off the counseling.

I saw Dr. Sparks for a month by myself, and then Raul saw him for a month by himself. Then we came back together for counseling.

Raul shared with the doctor that he was bothered by the fact that he had not bonded with Kim. "I'm afraid if I play with Kim, it will make Mary unhappy and I just can't do that to her," he said. "I can't help but feel that Mary is suffering from being displaced by Kim's adoption."

"How has the rest of the family bonded with Kim?" Dr. Sparks asked.

"Very well. We all love her, even Mary." I answered.

Dr. Sparks explained, "Raul, it takes a long time to bond with an older adopted child. Don't worry about loving her at this point. Can you just concentrate on making her feel good about herself? That is what every child needs. If Kim is happy at your house, you could ruin her little life by not going through with the final adoption. Imagine how your other children would feel, even Mary.

They might wonder what would happen if they did not measure up ... would you decide to send them away?" Dr. Sparks questioned Raul.

Looking ashamed, Raul said, "No, of course not. I will try. I think I can do it."

As I related before, my life was not easy in Fort. Kim was demanding and had special needs and always wanted to be held. She had a low frustration level and screamed loudly, and would not be consoled. I was running from morning until late at night. I felt like the old woman who lived in a shoe and had so many children she didn't know what to do. I loved the kids, but I was sometimes filled with doubt as to whether I had taken on more than I could handle. I wanted and needed to spend more time with Mary, but it was difficult because Raul would not spend any time with Kim to free me up for time with Mary.

One noon time I had to run down town to buy a pair of dark trousers for Steve to wear in a school concert. I loaded our kids and a couple neighbor kids into the big old station wagon and off we went. It was a short trip. When we returned, there sat three year old Bruce on the front step with tears running down his face. I had left him! I sat down by Bruce and we both cried. I felt like such a bad mother that day, definitely like that old woman who lived in the shoe.

I could see trouble brewing in our family. Not between Mary and Kim, but between Raul and Kim. He seemed to resent her and the time I spent with her because of her problems. He often verbalized that I needed to spend more time with Mary and not Kim, and yet he would not offer in any way to help with Kim. He could not see that Kim had any special needs to be addressed. I decided that he had not bonded with Kim as yet, and it would take longer for that to happen. I needed to be patient.

Raul grumbled about the way things were moving ahead in the medical practice in Fort. He had been promised a partnership after one year and it was not forthcoming. He said the partners wanted to wait another year. "I am not going to wait around. What if next year comes and they say 'next year' again. They didn't keep their word so I'm going to look for another job."

I had made Fort Atkinson my home and had dug in as if we were going to live there forever. I was not happy about the thought of moving again, but I felt if Raul weren't happy, none of us would be happy. I was beginning to think of my husband as a person with a dark cloud hanging over his head, a person who might never be happy and always be filled with negative thoughts.

If I misplaced the keys, he just knew they were gone forever. If the kids misplaced a toy, he would remark that it was lost for good. If a patient of his struggled, he withdrew into himself until the patient improved. I spent lots of time and energy trying to cheer him up. We were so different. I had been raised to be positive and to have faith. I was the eternal optimist and Raul was forever the pessimist. We should have complemented each other, but it did not work out that way.

7

On the Move Again

Raul found a medical practice in Cuba City, Wisconsin with three other doctors. He liked the idea that he would be the main surgeon and also do general practice. Cuba City was a town with a population of 1,997. I figured after the eight of us moved there, they surpassed the 2000 mark. We bought a big house with an acre on the outskirts of town, where there were five houses and about twenty kids. Behind our house were pastures with horses. Our kids thrived in Cuba City from day one. They were welcomed by the other kids and seemed to feel right at home. Mary and Kim seemed fascinated with the horses practically in our back yard. I took longer to adjust. I missed my friends in Fort Atkinson. I longed for my neighbors and the close proximity to Madison. I felt that Fort Atkinson with 10,000 people, had more to offer.

Raul was now communicating much better with me, and he insisted that we end our sessions with Dr. Sparks in Madison, now 80 miles away instead of 30. "I am all well," he insisted.

"We were just getting into the heart of the matter," I countered. He refused to go anymore, so I went a couple of times by myself.

"I'm sorry that Raul is opting out. I think we were just getting to where he could have made some real progress, and your marriage could have been greatly improved. Any changes you currently see probably won't last, because he still doesn't have insight into his problem," Dr. Sparks said.

Dr. Sparks forecasted correctly. Within a few months without therapy Raul slipped into his old ways. He complained about the way I laughed, the way I fixed my hair, the way I cooked, the way I mothered. If the kids caught a cold, he would ask me, "How could this happen? What did you do? Didn't you make them wear their jackets?" He criticized the fact that I went out after dinner to play a ball game with the kids before I washed the dishes.

There didn't seem to be much he liked about me. But I remember what Dr. Sparks said. He said, "Raul puts you down, Gayle, thinking it will make him feel better about himself. However, it doesn't work. Every time he puts you down he ends up feeling worse about himself. The worse he feels about himself, the more he puts you down."

It irritated him when one of the little neighborhood kids would ring the door-bell and ask, "Can Gayle come out to play?"

Our boys complained, "Dad will not listen. He starts to and then after you start talking he goes off on something different and you know he didn't hear you." He always had time for Mary; otherwise Raul seemed preoccupied. The only thing holding us together was sense of humor. Sometimes when things seemed darkest we would both break out laughing over something the kids said, and then for awhile things did not seem so bad.

Raul was a good doctor and a good surgeon. He loved his children and they knew it. He was proud of them and bragged about them to his patients and friends.

One Valentine's Day he bought me a lovely heart, filled with candy, and a fancy card … the first time ever. On it he had written, "I love you as much as I am capable of loving." Those words were probably as true a statement as he had ever made. If he did not learn anything else from Dr. Sparks, he learned that he did not have the capacity for true closeness and intimacy, at least with me.

Dr. Sparks told me on my last visit with him, "Gayle, if you are expecting to find happiness in your marriage, I don't believe you're going to find it. Perhaps you might find fulfillment in a career, but make sure you do something that will give you great satisfaction. I suggest that you place two sheets of paper inside a kitchen cupboard. On one you will jot down things you enjoy, on the other you will write things or tasks which you do not enjoy. After doing that for a month, look at them and see what you might like to pursue as a career." I did it. After a month it was pretty clear that I would be most satisfied working with people. I would not like to be an accountant, a banker, or work in a back room anywhere. I wanted to do something where I would be relating to people.

Since I was already an R.N., I decided to pursue a B.S. in Psychology. I had the idea that perhaps I could combine my nursing with psychology and work in mental health. Raul said, "I think it is dumb for you to go back to school at your age. If you do, don't expect me to help with the housework or anything else." Up until that time he had often helped with the laundry, cleaning or cooking. He drew the line at dishes. When I started school the kids began helping by doing their own laundry and taking turns on the dishes. On cleaning day they all pitched in to help. We played "Report for Duty." The kids would pretend they were in the army and would report for duty. I would give them a job to do. I was the commanding officer. They would salute and go about their assigned tasks. Mike especially liked this method of cleaning. Even Mary and Kim pitched in to help.

The girls were enrolled in pre-school in Platteville, a few blocks from the U.W. campus where I went to school (ten miles from Cuba City). Mary seemed to love the pre-school. She complained that Kim did not seem to take to it. It was as if she were embarrassed by Kim's lack of participation.

I scheduled all my classes around my schedule at home. During the second semester, I needed a class to happen at 6:00 P.M. Since I was majoring in psychology, I was particularly interested in a class called, "Current Topics in Psychology." I did not even read the class description, I just signed up. When I went to get my books, I was surprised to see that the book title was *Human Sexuality*. At my age I was taking a class on the birds and bees, I laughed. I was the oldest person in the class at age thirty-four! The rest of my classmates were between nineteen and twenty-two. The first night they gave us a test with one hundred-twenty-five questions. I missed thirteen, and decided I needed to be there. *Maybe I can figure out my own sex life.* It never ceased to amaze me what these eighteen and nineteen year olds thought about their parents' sexuality. When asked how often they thought their parents had sex, the most common answer was "Never!" (I was pretty sure that never was only at our house).

"Our son Mike asked his brother Steve, "Why is Mom going to school?"

"Because she wants to learn to help people with their problems," he explained.

"Oh good, she can help me with my math problems." Mike said.

"Is she going to be a cheerleader?" Bruce wanted to know.

"No," Matt told him, "She is too old to be a cheerleader."

The kids seemed tickled that I was going to school; becoming a student like they were. They often yelled to me as they went out the door, "Good luck on your test, Mom." Now I wasn't just Mom who did the laundry and cleaned the house. I was Mom who suffered through tests and homework like they did. Mary seemed to enjoy that she too was going to school. I think Kim liked it too, a little bit.

I joined a beginners' bridge club and made some new friends. One night I came home with new kitchen towels from bridge club. I told the kids, "I won the booby prize." As I walked into the kitchen I heard Bruce ask Matt, "What is a booby prize?"

"That's for having the biggest boobies." Matt always had an answer.

Mary was thriving in pre-school. Kim would not go into the classroom, would not even remove her coat for three weeks. She would stand at the space between the coat room and the classroom. She had a patient teacher who seemed to understand that when Kim was ready she would come in. One day Kim asked me "Why are only Mary's pictures on the refrigerator?" They were competitive.

"Because I don't have any Kim pictures; you won't go into the classroom and sit at your desk and make me some pictures to put on the fridge," I explained. The next day she entered the classroom, took off her coat, sat at her desk, and made pictures for the refrigerator. From then on she went to her desk. She was noticing that Mary pretty much had the spotlight.

At Christmastime I put up a string of letters spelling out "Merry Christmas".

Kim asked me, "What does it say?"

I told her, "It says 'Merry Christmas'"

"Why does it have to be Mary's Christmas?" she complained. How do you explain that to a three year old?

At age five Mary refused to wear dresses. I bought some really cute dresses for her to begin kindergarten. She said, "I hate them and I won't wear them. If you put them on me, I will take them off." And she did. By this time in the psychology of raising children, time-outs had become popular as the accepted form of discipline ... replacing spanking, which was becoming child abuse. The rule of thumb was to give a one minute time-out for each year of life. The first time I gave Mary a five minute time-out in her room it did not work out very well. When I went to release her, she was not there. She had taken off the screen and jumped out the front window, which was one and a half story high. Even at age five whenever she heard the word "no" she went into a tailspin. She did not seem to hear "no," it seems what she heard was "here is an obstacle which I need to get over."

It was at this age that I realized we had a problem with Mary. I knew she was spoiled and headstrong, and it was beginning to cause problems for the whole family. Raul stuck to his thought that Mary felt displaced by Kim. I felt he was spoiling her rotten ... he could not say no to her and stick to it. He would invariably give in.

Mary liked animals but would sometimes tantalize them. We had a cute little black puppy called "Muppy" who looked like a mop. Mary teased and terrorized Muppy. One day our Muppy got run over on the highway that ran by our house, and we had to have her put to sleep. Mary mourned that puppy for weeks. "I was mean to her. I want her to come back so I can be nice to her," she would wail. I would later call this the "Black Puppy Syndrome," the regret that often comes too late. Mary suffered from the "Black Puppy Syndrome" many times in her life.

Raul's mother died the year Mary was five. Since Raul's mother lived in the Philippines, Mary did not remember her. However, she was very upset by her death. She would creep into bed with me at night and say, "Promise me, Mama, that you will not die."

Knowing that I could not make such a promise, I would say, "Honey, Mama is not planning on dying. I am healthy. Grandma was sick." This happened at least a dozen times. While Mary treated people badly, I knew it was a surface thing. I knew that deep inside she cared for people, especially her family.

What is going on with this child? "*How can we help her to show her love and her hurt, not just her anger and hostility?*" I spent many a night in bed wrestling with this question. I would end up blaming the whole thing on the fact that she knew she could get her way by manipulating Raul. This was making her super spoiled, I thought. It was, in effect, a handicap for her within the family.

Neither Mary nor Kim enjoyed big gatherings. Kim was so shy that she clammed up in a group. Mary would become aggressive. On her eighth birthday we had a party and invited her friends, mostly neighborhood kids. When it came time to open presents, she opened the first one and said "Yuk, I hate that," and tossed it aside. She opened the next one and said, "Why did you buy me that?" She acted as if she did not know how to be nice, but I knew better. We had taught her.

I felt so bad for the children who had brought such nice gifts that I finally told the children, "Mary is not being nice, so she can't have a party today. Pick up your gifts and I will take you home." We never again invited friends to her birthday party. After that her birthdays were family affairs. It broke my heart to see her treat people like that.

Sometimes children would say to me, "Why is Mary so mean?" I frequently talked to her about how she treated people and she would say, "I don't like them. They're brats." I did lots of reading about strong-willed children and nothing I learned seemed to work. Little Mary was an expert at figuring out how to avoid discipline and how to manipulate people.

She was still a beautiful child. Big brown eyes, curly brown hair and pretty face. She and Kim played together, but I wondered how close they really were. It was as if Kim were Mary's puppet. Kim was no match for Mary's aggressiveness. Although I felt deep down that Mary would go to bat for her sister anytime she was needed.

Mary would often say, "Kim is too whiny."

Kim would say, "Mary is too bossy."

One evening Mary and Kim were playing and running around through the kitchen, through the living room, through the family room and then back through the kitchen, when Kim hit her head on the corner of the big buffet. She began to cry and a huge goose-egg developed on her forehead. When Mary saw the bump on Kim's head, she became hysterical. Kim, the injured one, immediately stopped crying and put her arm around Mary saying, "Its okay, Mary, don't cry!" Their closeness became obvious when one of them was hurt. In some ways they were like twins. They were only two months and eleven days apart. The difference was that they became twins at two years old and each had a set of problems and special needs with which they had been born.

Mary had a few good friends. One of her friends Anita lived on a farm and Mary frequently wanted to go there and spend the night. Anita also stayed overnight with us. If Mary liked a person she was usually nice to them, but one could lose their status very quickly if they crossed her. She was quick to say, "I do not like that girl anymore." Or, "I hate that teacher." Or, "I don't care about that snot." When she did have friends over, she treated her family badly, as if she thought by treating us badly she was displaying a badge of toughness to impress her friends.

Raul and I did not agree on the handling of Mary and Kim. He said that I babied Kim and I said that he spoiled Mary. I'm afraid we disagreed in front of them, which did not help anything. Raul resented it when Kim got something new. "She does not need new clothes. She can wear Mary's outgrown stuff." Raul frequently blamed Mary's bad behavior on Kim. He would say, "She is jealous of Kim, that's why she behaves that way."

I would say, "Raul, Mary is not the first child to have to adjust to a new sibling. It won't kill her. Give her a chance. Always giving in to her will only make it more difficult for her. She is very smart and she sees what is going on. She knows how to win," I pleaded. He couldn't bear the thought of Mary feeling badly about anything, and he could not see what this was doing to our family.

One day, while I was in a back bedroom making a bed, I heard this faint little scared cry, "Mama, help me." I ran to the family room. All I could see were Mary's little fingers grasping the window sill, as she was hanging by her fingertips out the second story back yard window. I dived for the window, grabbed her and pulled her in. She had leaned on the screen and it gave way. We both cried and held each other, I knowing that if she had fallen onto the pipes below, she could have been seriously injured. It was during moments like that when Mary seemed able to show her true feelings. Those were the times she became a normal frightened child. It was then that it seemed like she could let her defenses down and let me in. She would tell people after that incident "I almost died, didn't I, Mama?"

We had become good friends with the Creswick family in Cuba City. Ken was the hospital administrator. He and Raul built a friendship between our families. Ken and Purs (her real name was Priscilla) spent many hours at our house and we at theirs. We played cards, gardened, and went out for dinner. The Creswicks had a swimming pool which our kids loved to frequent. Their daughter Wendy was a regular at our house. She was near Mike's age. She told me, "There are so many kids at your house; it's like you're always having a party."

Our house was always full of kids, not just our six. They played ping-pong or we had a ball game out back. On one such occasion, when I was at bat, I hit a ball right through the sliding glass door of our downstairs. Raul was outside in no time. "Who did this?" he demanded.

All the kids looked at me. "I cannot tell a lie. I did it." I admitted, grinning like a guilty kid. "You need to grow up. How old are you anyway?" He seemed angry as he stomped back into the house.

"I'm sure glad it was you and not me!" one of the kids said.

The glass cost $250 to replace. I did not stop playing ball. We just moved home plate, so we were aiming at the pasture, not the house. I too was strong-willed and stubborn.

In 1974 the hospital decided to build a nursing home attached to the hospital, and Ken Creswick asked me if I would consider being the Director of Nursing. I was to graduate with my B.S. in Psychology in May, and this was December. I had planned that I would go into a mental health field after graduation, or work on my Masters and PhD. and become a psychologist. However, Ken was a good friend; I trusted him and thought he would be a good person to mentor me. I told him, "I will give you two years. I really want to go into mental health. So that is all I can promise you."

As usual, I filled my plate full to overflowing. I don't know what drove me to take on so much, but I loved a challenge. I was carrying eighteen credits at school. Mary and Kim were in first grade, Bruce in third grade, Mike in sixth grade, Matt in seventh and Steve in eighth. The boys were involved in sports and school. When I look back, I regret not having spent more time with Mary and Kim during this time in their lives. I will always wonder if it would have made a difference. *Why is hindsight so acute?*

I do remember taking a lengthy test in nursing school during our psych training. My results showed that I would always need new challenges to keep life interesting for me ...

Without realizing it, over the years I had let myself become dependent upon Raul. He wanted to keep it that way. He did not even want me to drive the nineteen miles to Dubuque, Iowa for shopping, without him.

One day I announced that I was going to drive back to Fort Atkinson, one hundred miles away, to see my friends. Raul objected. When I came out to get into the car, he had let the air out of all four tires. *This is going too far.* I got the tires inflated and away I went down the road, mad as could be. I don't know if Raul was being protective because he was afraid something would happen to me, or if he was afraid that I would become independent and not need him anymore. I could feel a spirit of independence rising in me. It's funny how this dependency thing had crept up on me. When I was eighteen I was full of independence. I had been on the downward spiral of dependence since our marriage.

Going back to college was my first attempt at losing my dependence on Raul. I had given everything I had to caring for Raul and the kids, with no thought about growing as a person. I had no regret about that. But going to school felt good and having a job felt good. Opening a nursing home, hiring the staff, writing the policies, ordering the supplies felt good. I felt challenged as a person. I felt successful. It became more than a fulltime job. It became my other life.

The kids had far too much time without me. I overcorrected. I went from dedicating myself totally to the family, to putting my job first and the family second. Of course, I could not see it at the time. The boys were so busy, I'm not sure they noticed I was gone so much. They were good boys and headed in a good direction. I was sure that Mary and Kim needed me, and I was not there for them. I think they were too young to even realize they needed me. When I was home, I was often tired and not as attentive to their needs as I had been when the boys were their age. I remember one evening when I was lying across the bed resting. Mary and Kim came in and were trying to tell me something. I went to sleep right in the middle of it. I often felt guilty and tried to make it up to them. Unfortunately, we rarely get a second chance to correct those kinds of mistakes.

Raul seemed ambivalent about my working. He was glad I was earning money, but he was not happy that dinner wasn't waiting for him when he got home. He wasn't happy about how the laundry piled up. He laughed at me when I sat down at 10:00 P.M. and studied until 2:00 A.M. "Do you fancy yourself a young coed?" he would tease. The kids pitched in though, and we managed. I think Raul was afraid of my independence. While our relationship was not any closer, I sensed he had a new respect for me now that I was not always at his beck and call.

During my junior year at the university, I entered the spring fiction contest. When I told the family they were all excited, except Raul. "So now you think you are an author," he laughed. It was clear to me that he did not want me to succeed. It was not clear to me *why* he did not want me to succeed. I won first place in the contest and got a check for $300 dollars. I waved it in front of his nose. I made a copy for framing. My picture was in the paper receiving the award. The sweet taste of success was enveloping me.

I would often say to him when we fought, "You know, Raul, I think we need a divorce. We are growing farther and farther apart and fighting more and more. This cannot be good for us or for the kids."

"Just what do you think you would do without me to bring home a paycheck?" he asked.

"I would get by just fine. I am a nurse, you know. I already have a job as Director of Nursing."

"How much is that paying you?"

"Enough for me. You would have to pay alimony and child support."

"You think you could live on that? You couldn't live high on the hog like we live now!"

"I don't care. There would be peace, and the fighting would go away."

"You're dreaming, Gayle. You don't live in the real world. Every couple fights like we do." *Did they?*

The spoiling of Mary became more prevalent with my reentry into the workplace. When her behavior was bad, Raul would make excuses for her. He would disagree with any discipline I would try. The boys would often say to him, "That's not fair, Dad. If that was one of *us*, you would not give in." He was a blind man to Mary's behavior. I will have to admit that sometimes I was just too tired to argue about it. I didn't know what was worse, letting him spoil her or arguing about it all the time.

8

The Spoiling War

Sometimes family life became so busy I tended to think that serious problems were simply everyday problems that all families experience. That's the way it was with us. When crises occurred, we would feel for a short time like there was something wrong with us. Then when it was over we would feel like we were just an average family with no more problems than anyone else. I think most of our friends thought we were a normal family, although I could be wrong. When it comes to family life, what is normal anyway? Is there some finite measure of a happy family?

There were lots of good times. Sunday evenings I would make enough dinner for an army so the kids could invite friends. Craig Weber was a regular Sunday evening guest. He was Steve's best friend and also a friend to the other boys. He would come into the kitchen and look at the spaghetti sauce and say, "This looks like enough for me, but what are the rest of you going to eat?" This red-haired, freckle-faced boy was a favorite at our house.

Our Steve was a good student and would "hold class" most weekday evenings. Craig, some of the neighbors, some of our kids, and always Kim, would gather around the big table and do their homework. Some would get help with their homework from Steve. I can still hear Steve shout at Craig who had wondered out to the living room to watch TV, "Craig, get in here. We're not finished."

I will always be grateful that we lived in a small town for those eight years. We always knew where the kids were. If they did something wrong, we would get a call. The teachers and principals knew all the students, and would call us if there was something we needed to know. Maybe it was because I grew up in a small town that I felt good about it. Our whole family formed strong friendships in Cuba City.

There was something very comforting about how the townspeople pulled together for other families when tragedy struck. I learned that people who resided in small towns may not have had fine restaurants and lots of activities or opportunities, but there was much socializing. People got together to play cards. They faithfully followed all the high school sporting events. There were many parties. There were many churchgoers. They seemed to reach out more than their city counterparts. It was much like Wray, Colorado where I grew up.

As Mary advanced in school, the problems at home grew. She still refused to wear a dress at any time. She was a tomboy. She was rough and tough. Mary did not like anything frilly or feminine. Sometimes I could use reverse psychology to get her to do something. "Mary, please do not wear that blue shirt. I don't like it." It was for sure she would wear the blue shirt.

One night we were out to dinner with our friends Elsie and Paul. Elsie was my tall Swedish friend. At dinner she said, "Raul, why do you spoil Mary so much? Don't you see that it is hurting her?"

"I am not spoiling her," he said.

"Raul, I have been there and have seen how you let her have whatever she wanted, after Gayle had said she could not have it."

"Why is everyone against Mary? She got all fouled up because of Kim's adoption. No one understands this but me"

"Raul, that is not true." I said.

Before we could continue the conversation, Raul glared at us, got up from the table, went out into the car, and drove off leaving us at the restaurant out in the country. I sat there with my mouth open at his response. It was the first time anyone but me had pointed out to him the seriousness of the spoiling.

My friend Elsie said, "Gayle, what are you going to do? This is serious."

"I don't know, Elsie, and I know it cannot go on forever."

Mary's behavior was affecting each member of the family in a different way. Steve, ever the diplomat, seemed to like both the girls and played with them and tried to reason with them. Once in awhile he would get fed up and talk to me about Mary's behavior. Matt was fast becoming disenchanted with Mary getting her way and he would engage Raul in arguments about why he gave Mary so much money, and why he always gave into her, and why there were different rules for Mary. Mike, who never liked fighting and unpleasantness, would go out of his way to try to keep peace among all members of the family. He often played with both girls.

When I thought of Mary I was reminded of the nursery rhyme, "There was a little girl, who had a little curl, right in the middle of her forehead. When she was good, she was very, very good, and when she was bad she was horrid." It fit.

Bruce, who was just two years older than Mary and Kim, would enter into open battle with Mary when she crossed him, which was often. Bruce was in a hard place. He was three years younger than Mike, so was unable to do every thing his big brothers could do. He was often left to play with Mary and Kim, which would result in fighting for the power and control. Bruce would often be chastised by Raul for fighting with Mary. "She is two years younger than you," Raul would say to him.

"Yeah, but she is meaner," he would reply.

The first instance of Mary having reportable trouble at school was in fourth grade. The teacher had reprimanded another student and Mary did not think it was warranted. She verbally stood up to the teacher. Mary would not back down and we were called to school. I was surprised that Mary would do this at school. When I tried to talk to her about it, she kept saying, "The teacher was wrong, and I'm not going to let her get away with it. I will do it again if she does it to some-one else." The more we discussed it the more stubborn she became.

Mary made other friends at school, but Anita was her closest friend. She already had a well-developed sense of standing up for her friends. This was a trait that would follow her into adulthood. She often stood up for people, some whom she should not have defended. This caused her undue problems in her life and it sometimes made problems for me as well.

The danger of writing about a family problem is that one may get the impres-sion that we had a terrible life all the time. Not so. When I look back as if I am looking at a movie of our life I see a bustling, happy family with lots of love for each other. Then I see blips on the movie screen depicting our crises. When you are in the middle of a crisis, you tend to feel as if life is impossible. When it passes you think, "*We made it over this one. We will be fine. Things will get better.*" Of course, I'm sure we had more "blips" than the average family.

Our marital problems were heating up. I wanted so to have a loving relation-ship with Raul. However, it was heading the wrong way. I had lots of love to give and he didn't want it. I did not realize it but I guess I was a sitting duck for a love relationship outside my marriage. As it happened I fell in love with a good friend who was also a sitting duck. Two married, sitting ducks. Not a good situation, but it may have been a life-saving one for me. From this relationship I got back my self-esteem, got up enough nerve to end a bad marriage, and to move away and to go on with my life.

Toward the end of our marriage the fighting with Raul became physical. One Christmas season evening I was preparing a spaghetti dinner. Raul and I got into a fight. Most of our fights were about how to raise the kids, how to spend/save money, lack of sex in our marriage, and about how to deal with Mary's behavior.

This particular night it was about my generosity with money. Whenever we talked about money Raul referred to it as "his money".

"I want to help my niece who is trying to get her college education," I said.

"Why you?" He asked.

"Because she needs it and we have it," I said.

"You are so generous with my money." He raised his voice.

"How do you figure it's *your* money?"

"I'm the one who earned it."

"And who manages the family, the house, and all the errands so you can do that? And who coached you and quizzed you so you could pass your exams, so you could make money? Doesn't that count for something? I thought it was *our* money!" I was out of breath.

"It is still my money because I earned it."

"We'll see how much of it is yours when we go to divorce court." I spouted.

He walked over to me as I was carrying a pot of hot water to the stove to cook the spaghetti noodles. He whacked me in the face with the back of his hand. My nose shot blood all over and I dropped the pan of water on the floor. The kids came running. Mary and Kim began crying when they saw the blood. I was so afraid of traumatizing them that I faked calmness, "I'm okay, and it's just a little bloody nose. Everything is okay. Mama's not hurt." Internally I was devastated. Raul had never laid a hand on me before. I lay awake that night. *You always said if a man ever laid a hand on you, you would leave him. What are you going to do now?* Raul was very apologetic the next day and was kind and gentle to all of us for several days afterward, until I almost forgot about it.

Raul and I were like two acquaintances living together. Two people who were not that fond of each other. Raul could not stand to be touched in bed, so I had begun sleeping on the sofa in the living room. I slept better. It actually relieved some of the tension between us. There were no sexual advances for him to have to reject, and I was not feeling rejected. I don't know if the boys ever noticed that I slept on the sofa for five years. They never asked me about it. Mary asked about it much later.

I was building up a lot of anger at Raul for the way he gave into Mary. We fought constantly about it. I felt he should back me up if I doled out a discipline. A typical example which happened daily was: "Raul, I told Mary she could not go to Anita's, because she didn't do her chores. And now you said she could go."

"Well, she wants to go," he replied.

"Why can't you say 'no', if it would be good for her?" I asked.

"I just can't," he said.

"You are ruining her," I accused.

"You are too hard on her," he countered.

"Raul, please try to see. You make the other kids do what I say, why not Mary?" I continued in a louder voice.

"She has had it rough," he tried.

"She has had it easier than any of our other kids." I raised my voice.

And so it went. The arguments became more frequent as the marriage tumbled downhill. It was like sledding down those hills in Colorado. I would be going faster than I wanted to but could do nothing to stop the sled. In between our arguments we looked, felt, and sounded like the All-American Family. It's hard to believe, but that's the way it was.

I was learning so much at my new job. I was part-time at first, until I was graduated from U.W. It was exciting to be learning all I could learn about nursing homes and their regulations. I visited other homes in the area to learn what I could. I memorized the codes. Of course, I had doubts. *Could I really manage such an important job? These residents were going to depend upon me for a lot in the home stretch of their lives. Could I do it? What if I let them down? What if I hire the wrong people?* These were the questions that haunted me in the wee small hours of the morning when I couldn't sleep.

I had been a leader in high school and in nurses' training. In the past when I worked, it seemed that I had always landed a job where I was in charge of something or a group of employees. It always went well. Those thoughts comforted me during my periods of doubtfulness. *I can make it*, I prayed.

Raul became well-established in the area. He was a good surgeon and meticulous in his work, which was sometimes an irritant to his associates. He would take time to make it perfect. Sometimes that made for longer time in the operating rooms for his assistants.

I would occasionally hear gossip about his womanizing. When I would press for details none were forthcoming. I was busy in my own career at this point and I was falling in love. After the episode in Fort Atkinson with Jill, I had lost a big part of the love I felt for Raul. I had come to know that Raul would not be true to our marriage. I did not feel obligated to be true to it anymore myself. I felt separated from him even though we occupied the same house. I wasn't sure exactly where this marriage was going, but we were moving toward it pretty fast.

9

The Marriage Quakes

One night we went to dinner with friends Kim and Sandy. Kim was the nephew of our friends Purs and Ken. Kim was a guy who could be one of the nicest people, or he could be a real donkey. This particular night he was giving Sandy a hard time all evening. Sandy was a piano teacher, an EMT and an active person in Cuba City. She had beautiful hair, a pretty face and a nice olive complexion. She was a little overweight, although she always looked like a million dollars.

I was getting sick of hearing Kim put her down. It reminded me of the way Raul put me down. *Why do some guys think they are so perfect?* As we were driving home and were about a half mile from our house Kim said to Sandy, "If you would lose about forty pounds and get your degree, I might be attracted to you."

Sandy did not say anything. I was livid and could not contain myself any longer. "Kim," I snipped. "Maybe Sandy will lose forty pounds and maybe she *will* get her degree. And then maybe she will look around and say, "What am I doing with this asshole?"

We were pulling into the driveway at our house. Kim was furious at me, "Shut up, Gayle," he yelled. "Handle your own marriage problems first, and then maybe you can advise me about mine."

Raul was furious at me for interfering. He yelled at me, "Gayle, keep your mouth shut. It's none of your business."

I could not stop, even though I knew Raul was right. I identified with their situation because it was much like Raul's and mine. When I got out of the car, I took off my high heel and threw it at Kim. I think he was ready to come after me, but I ran into the house.

Raul followed on my heels and started yelling at me. "Who do you think you are? I didn't think you were that stupid."

"I couldn't help it. No man should treat a woman like that. Sandy does not deserve that. Someone had to tell him and Sandy wasn't saying anything. You men think you can put a woman down any time you want. I'm sick of it!" I yelled back. I had obviously transferred my feeling about us onto Kim and Sandy.

Now I was upset at Raul. I grabbed the keys off the counter and started running downstairs to the garage. "I'm getting out of here." I said.

"No you're not!" he yelled.

I continued into the garage with Raul on my heels. He got in front of me and pushed me. I fell backwards over the lawn mower and hit my head on the floor. I must have temporarily lost consciousness, because when I came to, he was booting me down the stairs and back into the house. I could not register what was happening. "Wake up, Bitch," he was saying. When he saw that I was awake, he left me and went upstairs.

I lay there for a long time, unable to take in what had just happened. I knew I was wrong to enter into Kim and Sandy's quarrel. But did I deserve this? I was hurting all over. Slowly I began moving myself to see if I were broken anywhere. Outside of being dizzy, I seemed to be okay. I crawled into Steve and Matt's bedroom. Matt was staying overnight with a friend, so I crawled into his bed. I did not cry. I was numb. Eventually, I went to sleep. In the morning I examined my body which was full of bruises, but nothing I could not cover. I would not have to explain them to anyone. Thank God the kids slept through this episode.

After a fight like that I was filled with sorrow for our kids. They deserved better than battling parents. I would spend extra time with Mary and Kim trying to make it up to them for having to live in this fighting household.

This event marked the beginning of the end of the marriage for me. I figured that if I cared enough to be angry, then I still cared, and it was probably not over yet. And I was still angry. I figured once I became too numb to become angry I would not care what Raul did or said. Then it wouldn't matter.

At a hospital picnic ballgame I slid into second base and hurt my foot. I could not put weight on it, so Raul took me to the hospital for an X-Ray. He did not think it looked like it was broken, so I went home and put ice on it. He lectured me, "You need to grow up. You are forty years old and have no business sliding into second base, or even playing ball for that matter!"

The next night we went to a party at our little Country Club, which was kind of the center of social activity for Cuba City ... it was also open to the public. Raul and I got into an argument. I was so mad that I went out the door to walk home. I did not want him to bring the car and try to pick me up, so I walked across a plowed up field the mile or so home, sinking into the moist dirt up to my knees. My injured foot was killing me. I arrived home and put my feet into the bath tub. What a muddy mess I was. My foot was throbbing and I was crying, not so much about the foot as about the broken relationship and the hopelessness of it all.

On Monday morning the radiologist read my X-Ray and called and told me that my heel was broken. Raul put a cast on it that day. I was still mad at him and barely speaking to him. I think he would have liked to put a cast on my mouth to shut me up.

I admit to being assertive and spunky. Sometimes I thought "if only I could have been a passive person, maybe the marriage could have been saved." The very idea of that was distasteful to me. I was coming out from under a dependency role, and was not about to let someone smash me down again.

After another party night at Cole Acres, we were invited to breakfast at another couples house. (I will not tell you their names ... it was a small town!) We knew them quite well. It did not take me long to realize that I had been set up. I had always been naïve about some things. It took me awhile to realize that the man was coming on to me. Raul was sitting by the woman and they were getting very friendly. I felt uncomfortable and told the man outright that I was not playing around. When I saw Raul's hand go up the woman's leg under her dress, I jumped up and said, "That's all folks. I am out of here!"

I remember that the road to our house was all ice. I took off my heels and skated and slipped and slid all the way home. I felt giddy. *That S.O.B. cannot hurt me anymore. I don't feel jealous. I don't feel angry. I don't feel hurt. I almost feel sorry for him that he is resorting to making out with that homely woman, and she is homely, and not a bit sexy in my opinion. Man, he is scraping the bottom of the barrel.* I had no idea what transpired that night after I left their house and I had no curiosity about it. We never talked about it. I knew the fat lady had sung. This marriage was over.

At this time I was taking a class called Psychology of Personal Adjustment at college. This was the advanced class. We delved into each other pretty deeply. We each had a partner with whom we were given exercises to do and discuss. It was in one of these sessions that my partner Vern questioned me about the marriage, of which by now he had heard plenty. I didn't realize it, but I spent a lot of time dwelling on playing the victim role.

"Gayle, what I do not understand, is why you like all the pain."

"I don't like the pain. I hate it." I answered.

"Well you must like it or you would have done something about it," he replied.

That was an eye-opener for me. That very day I made an appointment to see Attorney Brown. He had been referred to me by a classmate. She had used him for her divorce and said he was fair and easy to work with. I went to see him and asked him all about divorce. He asked me, "Are you in any danger?"

"I don't think so." I answered.

"I am going to give you my home phone number so you can reach me at any time. If it becomes an emergency, you can call me." I thanked him and left. On the way home it hit me that we were almost at the end of the line. I was filled with dread about the days ahead. I also had another emotion: relief at making the hard decision.

A few days after my appointment with the attorney, I was talking with our oldest son Steve. I could usually share feelings with him. He was a good listener and seemed to understand far beyond his years.

"Mom, I think you and Dad need to get a divorce," he surprised me.

"You think so?"

"Yes. I don't think this fighting is good for any of us."

"How do you think the rest of the kids would feel?" I ventured. "I have actually spoken to an attorney about it"

"I think they would be relieved that the fighting was over," he said.

"I've thought a lot about it, Steve, but I can't quite figure out the details." I said.

"I have heard about people staying together for the kids' sake," he said. "I don't think that makes any sense. We love both of you, and we would not want to lose either of you, but don't do us any favors by staying together."

"What about Mary? What do you think this will do to her?"

"All I know is that if Dad keeps spoiling her she doesn't have a chance."

"I need to do some more soul searching about the details. There are things like living space and money that I have not figured out," I told him. *It's pretty bad if your teen-ager has to tell you that you need a divorce.*

On graduation day from the university, Raul acted as if he were proud of me. I graduated summa cum laude. The kids seemed proud. They knew they had played an important part. I never could have done it without their help and support. Against all odds, we had done it. No one could take it away from me. Not even Raul! We had a nice celebration at a local restaurant.

Once in awhile Raul would surprise me. On my forty-third birthday, we had planned to go out with another couple. We were going to meet at the Elmo Club just outside of town, and from there on to Dubuque. When we arrived at Elmo, there were lots of friends there and I began visiting with them. It took quite awhile before someone explained that this was a surprise birthday party … for me! I had never been surprised like that. We had a prime rib dinner and a great time. Usually Raul did not even remember my birthday. *What was this? Now that it's over, is he starting to like me?*

Mary was becoming a bigger challenge. If we were going to the grocery store and wanted her to go with us, she would say, "No, I don't want to go."

So we would get in the car to go and she would stand in back of the car so we could not leave. I would get out and remove her and take her into the house and by the time I would be in the driver's seat again, she would be out there again behind the car, so we could not go. If Raul was home he would not take a stand on this and make her stay or go. This would happen dozens of times. It would make the other kids angry. For the life of me I was never able to figure out why she did that. It seemed she had a tug-of-war going on in her head.

Other times Mary would be aggressive to her older brothers. If they took action against her, Raul would admonish them, "She is much younger than you, and you shouldn't fight with her." In truth, she was picking on them. It was as if she had diplomatic immunity when Raul was around.

The rumors that Raul had a girlfriend kept finding their way back to me. Either my informants didn't know who it was or they were not brave enough to tell me. "You know I don't care anymore." I would tell them. "If he has a girlfriend, let me know who it is and I will tie a big yellow bow around him and deliver him to her!" I don't think they realized that I was serious.

We always attended the athletic events in Cuba City. Our whole family enjoyed sports. At a football game one night where our three older boys were playing football, Raul and I were sitting on the bleachers. Mary and Kim had been given money to spend at the concession stand. After Mary had spent her money, she came around, wanting more money. I said, "No, you have spent your money." Raul gave her more money and, of course, when that was gone she came back for more. Again I said "no." He eventually gave in again. I think he gave in because she was getting loud and demanding, which embarrassed him. She even used the four letter word when I said no. I was still fuming when we got home. I was mad at her for keeping on until she got her way and I was mad at Raul for giving into her. I tried to give Mary a time-out in her room. She ran outside and I could not catch her. So I turned on Raul.

"I hope you're happy with what you have created. You have created a child who thinks if she throws enough of a fit, she can get anything she wants. What will it be like when she is a teen-ager?"

"It is your fault she is that way. You baby Kim and you are too hard on Mary," he yelled.

"You are crazy!" I out-yelled him.

At this he took off his shoe with the big heel (he wore them to make him taller) and began chasing me. He hit me once. Bruce, Kim, and even Mary were crying. It was a bad scene for anyone to see, especially our kids. Raul stopped when I went to the phone. I think he thought I was going to call the police. I called my attorney and told him that we had an emergency situation and I needed to proceed with the divorce. He asked "Do you want me to call the police?"

"No, I think this emergency has passed." I agreed to meet him in his office the next day. I told Raul that I was filing for divorce. I don't think he believed me, because I had threatened it too many times in the past year.

Since the above event happened over a disagreement about Mary, I think she always carried with her the feeling that she caused the divorce. I tried to explain to all of the kids that there were many problems between Raul and me and our problems had nothing to do with our kids. However, I knew if there was to be any solution to the handling of Mary, it would not come about with our staying together and arguing about her behavior.

The next day I met with Attorney Brown. I was adamant that I did not want to have a messy divorce. The kids had been through enough.

"I don't want alimony and I don't want any of his retirement money. I just want child support. If I took half of the retirement money (which my attorney said I deserved) it would make him furious and cause more fighting. After all, he thought it was all *his* money. I've been through enough. I want to be done with this marriage," I said.

"We will have the County Sheriff deliver the notification to Raul," he explained.

"That will not be necessary. I've been telling him for a long time that I was going to get a divorce. I told him to expect it. I will give the notice to him myself."

"Are you sure? Sometimes there is quite a reaction," he answered.

"It's okay. He will probably continue living there until he can find a place to live. So it's not like I am kicking him out into the street," I explained.

"That works for some couples, but not many. Only you know what will work for you," he sounded doubtful.

I arranged to give Raul the papers when there was no one else at home.

"What the heck is this?" he asked, as I handed them to him.

I was totally unprepared for his reaction when he looked at them. We were in the family room. He literally picked up a recliner and threw it, breaking a leg on it. He was not a big guy and I had never thought of him as strong. I was totally shocked.

"You don't know what you're doing. You can't get along without me. How are you going to manage six kids by yourself?" He was furious. I had told him I was going to file.

"I don't plan to manage them by myself. You and I are getting a divorce. You are not divorcing the kids. They're going to spend plenty of time with you."

"So what happens now?" he asked when he had calmed down.

"I'm not kicking you out," I explained. "You can stay here until you find a place, if there's no fighting. Our kids have been through enough of our fights. I'll go my way and you go yours. You can date in the open now; you won't have to skulk around."

"You mean I have to move?"

"Eventually."

"Why don't *you* move out?"

"I will, if that is what you want. You would then be managing the kids, the house, the shopping, and the cleaning … if you think you can …"

"Never mind," he said quickly.

"My thought is that we tell the kids together in a calm way and assure them that the main way their life is going to change is that they won't have to put up with our fighting. Once they know they will still have access to both of us, they will be okay."

Some of the kids were obviously upset. Mike seemed very upset. Mary cried and said, "It's all my fault, I know it is." We both tried to assure her that it was between Raul and me. The family, as they had known it, was about to end. Some of them voiced that they did not want to lose either one of us. All in all they seemed to handle it pretty well. Kim seemed relieved. Mary was the one who showed the most emotion over it. She begged me not to get the divorce. "I'll be so good, Mom." The "Black Puppy Syndrome" again.

The next week Raul and I were driving to Platteville. He said, "If you go through with this divorce, I will kill myself."

I was ready for this because I suspected he might say that. I had spoken to my Personal Adjustment class at school about how to respond to it.

I said, "That is your problem, Raul. If that is the legacy you want to leave your children, I cannot stop you." Of course I prayed that he would not do anything so foolish, because I knew I would blame myself. I figured he was trying to hang on the only way he knew. He never mentioned it again.

We maintained the "live in" relationship for a few months. I kept telling him, "You have to start looking for a place. I would show him ads in the paper, but he showed no interest. Maybe he thought if he stayed long enough I would change my mind.

The pressure on me was much less after filing. To me the decision was the hardest part. With Raul continuing to live at the house, it was a way of easing out of the divorce, a way which I felt was better for the kids. My friends couldn't believe how we were doing this divorce. We would still go out for dinner once in awhile. I am sure we were the topic of every dinner table in Cuba City. I could only imagine the conversations, "Are they splitting, or aren't they?" I remembered Dr. Sparks' words, "You two would probably get along fine if you weren't married."

After a few months, I could see that Raul needed to move. And I could see that he was not going to do it himself. I found a little house available in Cuba City, and while he was at work I moved him into it. With the help of a friend, we got it all organized, made the bed, bought food for him, and arranged for the kids to take turns staying with him, so he would not be lonely. When he came home that evening, I told him, "Raul, you do not live here anymore. I found a nice little place for you and moved you in."

"You what?" he asked.

"You now have your own little place in Cuba City."

He took it pretty well, even had a little chuckle. Then I literally took him over there, gave him the keys and a couple of kids and left. I'm sure the news of this traveled very fast around town. News travels at the speed of light in a small town. If there is a down side to small town living, that is it.

There did not seem to be any fall-out to speak of as far as our household. I actually slept in the bed for the first time in five years. I listened to the radio and I read. It felt good. I kept waiting for the depression to settle in. I had read about the feeling of isolation and aloneness that the newly divorced are supposed to feel. I didn't feel it. I felt the loneliness and depression while we were married. Five years ago when I used to sleep with Raul, I could not read in bed because he did not like the light. I could not listen to the radio because it bothered him. Now I could read all night if I wanted to! The kids and I got along fine. Even Mary seemed more settled. Raul dropped out to see them frequently and they visited him at his house.

The only negative was that I often did not have a partner for going out to dinner. I had girlfriends and we would sometimes go to Dubuque or Madison. I could not imagine having a date or how the kids would take it if I did have one.

Through my ties at the university I met a couple single professors whom I dated. I was on my way to meet an art professor for a drink in Platteville for my first outing with a male since the divorce. My car met my son Steve's car as he was driving home from basketball practice. It was snowing a wet snow. We stopped to greet each other. "Mom, where are you going? He asked.

"I'm going to Platteville. I have a date." I told him and watched for his reaction.

"Who with?' he wanted to know.

"With an art professor from the university," I answered. "We are meeting at The Timbers for a drink and dinner."

"Mom, you need your windshield cleaned." He hopped out and was wiping the snow off my windshield. As he was cleaning he was singing, "My mom has a date, my mom has a date, my mom has a date." He seemed to be getting a kick out of it. I was so relieved that he was not upset about his mom going out with another man. What a kid! His brothers and sisters seemed okay with it too. Matt wanted to know what kind of car he drove.

Mary said, "He will not be *my* dad!" I assured her it was just a date.

I was the one not okay with it. It felt strange to be dating at my ripe old age. It seemed to me that older men got serious too fast. After a few dates my art professor started talking about getting married. He said, "We could buy a place between Cuba City and Platteville and make a gym for the boys. It could be lots of fun."

"I'm definitely not ready for that," I answered. That scared me. I drew back quickly from that relationship. *When I date others I feel as if I am masquerading as a teen-ager. It feels strange. What am I doing here?*

My biggest fear at that time was that I would make the same mistake I had made the first time ... and marry someone with whom I was not compatible. I had many friends that had repeated their first mistake. I also knew that nurses tended to marry someone they thought they could rescue. I definitely did not want to try that again. Been there. I had my radar out to pick up clues ... if I thought they needed rescuing, I ran the other way.

Raul started dating right away. Believe it or not, he came to me for advice about dating! And I helped him! I was truly out of love with him. I wanted him to find someone and to be happy. He was dating Charlotte, and we invited her to Thanksgiving dinner. I did not want the kids to feel pulled in two directions, and I did not want them to think that I would be hurt by their dad being with another woman. When I met her, I liked her. I could not help but wonder and hope that they were more compatible than Raul and I had been.

After Thanksgiving dinner, Char offered to help with the dishes. Raul said to her, "Honey, you do not have to help with the dishes." Maybe they both saw the daggers that I sent to him, because she did help with the dishes.

The nerve. Not once in our twenty years of marriage had he spoken like that to me. I was ticked off that he was treating me like a house maid, when I thought I was pretty generous of spirit inviting her to dinner! *Didn't have to help with the dishes?*" He might as well say, "Let Gayle the Maid wash the dishes." I repeated this unbelievable phrase over and over to myself.

We did not fight over the terms of the divorce, especially the financial arrangements. I was sure his attorney told him he was getting off easy. After all, he had it good. He was going to pay $300 per month in child support and I did not touch his retirement, even though my attorney told me I was entitled to half of it. I was capable of working and had a good job, I reasoned. Many times over the years I regretted not being more assertive in the finances of the divorce.

10

Uprooting the Family

After Raul moved out, I began thinking: *There is no reason for me to stay in Cuba City. I don't have any of my family within 1900 miles. I love Arizona where my brothers Steve, Bud, Jay, Dean, Leo, and my sister Joan live with their families. It would be good for the kids to have some extended family nearby.* However, I did not tell the kids yet. I did talk to Raul about it. He seemed to like the idea because he could then move back into the house. I had a feeling that Char and he would be married before too long. I made up my mind to move to Arizona and began looking for a job. I wondered if she were up to mothering Mary, because I felt sure when the kids were given a choice, Mary would choose to stay with her dad.

It was a difficult decision job wise. I loved my job at Cuba City Medical Center. Our nursing center had experienced excellent ratings with the state. We had developed a wonderful, caring staff. I loved the residents who lived in our nursing center. Work was fun. The Administrator, Ken Creswick, was the greatest mentor. He taught me much about management. He also taught me to be patient and to think out decisions completely before leaping. He taught me to believe in myself. *Could I leave all this?* Because of impending changes at the hospital and because I felt the need to start over, I said to myself, *If you are ever going to leave, this would be the time to do it.* I was so eager to begin my new life that I gave my notice before securing a job in Arizona.

Through a friend in Wisconsin I found out about a job in Arizona. I applied for it. I received a call to go to Des Moines for a day of pre-employment psychological testing at an industrial psychology firm there. I had not been through anything like that before, and I was a little uneasy.

I arrived in Des Moines in the afternoon and had instructions to stay at a specific hotel and eat at Guido's restaurant. I decided that eating at Guido's was part of my psychological test because the maitre d' seated me in a corner booth and then no one approached me for one hour. *They are testing my patience. How long would a patient person be expected to wait for service, before taking action? I decided upon one hour.*

After one hour I approached the maitre d' and said, "Excuse me, sir. I was seated an hour ago and have not received any service in that time." He literally jumped and apologized all over, brought me a complimentary bottle of wine. Then I had to ask myself ... *is this another test to see if I am a drinking woman?* I had one glass of wine, deciding that few could fault me for that.

The testing included a half-day written exam. Then I met with an industrial psychologist named Tom Tenton in the afternoon, who asked me more questions. One question he asked me was: "Do you ever cuss?"

I hesitated and then replied, "I have been known to say a few cuss words when riled."

"Then I will be honest with you," he said, "You may not get this job. Some of these retirement communities have very fundamentalist leanings and would frown upon a person who uses cuss words."

"How do they feel about lying?" I asked. He grinned slightly.

Evidently I passed muster, because I got a call to go to for an interview with the personnel committee of the Board of Directors for the position of Health Care Administrator in Tempe, Arizona, at Friendship Village of Tempe. I was filled with fright at the thought of interviewing for a job that was bigger than anything I had ever done. I met with the committee on a Saturday morning. I felt good chemistry with them. They hired me ... cuss words and all.

Friendship Village was a beautiful life care senior community that offered independent living and skilled nursing on one campus. It was a huge new place that was not yet completed. Eventually it would have two hundred-fifteen apartments, one hundred-twenty nursing beds, and three hundred-ten garden homes. I was excited and felt fortunate to secure the position. Every once in awhile I would think, *Wow, mama, you did it!*

Raul and I sat down together and explained to our kids that I would be moving to Arizona and that each of them could make a choice to stay in Cuba City or move to Arizona. Guess who spoke up first? It was Mary. "I'm moving to Arizona!" she said without hesitation. I was shocked but pleased. I believed if she lived away from Raul she had a chance to straighten out, but I could not understand her quick decision to come with me. I finally came to the conclusion that in her heart she knew all the spoiling was not good for her. I had thought surely she would want to stay with her dad who gave her everything she wanted.

Steve, who was in pre-med at UW Madison, would stay in Wisconsin and complete his studies. Matt was currently attending college at UW Platteville and would stay, but said he wanted to come to Arizona when he got out of school. Mike was a senior in high school and would stay to complete high school, and then he would come to Arizona. Bruce, Mary and Kim, the three younger ones, would go with me.

Good-byes were hard. Our family was breaking into two pieces, which would now be 1900 miles apart. We stood outside at 5:00 A.M. on November 19, saying our good-byes. It was dark and cold and the wind was howling. I would miss these three older boys. I would miss Cuba City. I knew the boys would do fine without me ... they were good kids and they were strong. I cried off and on all the way to Arizona. We were a subdued group by the time we arrived in Tempe. I could tell my crying upset the kids, especially Mary, who kept quizzing me as to why I was crying. "I just feel sad about leaving your brothers," I told her.

"Me too," she said.

I found a cute house in Tempe, five minutes from work. My job was new and scary because my new boss wouldn't even talk to me. He showed me my office on Monday and then did not speak to me for the next week. I went home feeling down every day, thinking that I had made a huge mistake. "My new boss doesn't like me!" I would complain to the kids. Everyone else at Friendship Village was friendly. It was a demanding job. I often worked ten to twelve hours a day. After the first week I decided that I would have to somehow get through to this guy. I began speaking to him every day and even carried on one-sided conversations with him. After one week he started reciprocating with conversations of his own. It worked. He slowly became friendlier and we began working well together. I think he finally realized that I was there to help him.

Bruce, Mary and Kim were having trouble adjusting to our new life. When school began none of them liked it. Whenever Mary was stressed out about something, she acted out more. To top it off, when I had to say no to one of her demands (she rarely *asked*); her response was more intense than in Cuba City. She did not have her dad around to give in to her. I'm sure it was a painful realization for her. I fully believed that her behavior would greatly improve after awhile. I realized we were engaged in a power struggle. Instead of the struggle between Raul and I about how to deal with Mary, it was a struggle between Mary and me.

Mary was somewhat like a wild horse captured and brought into the corral. She would take a run at the fence but could find no way out. She tried everything she knew to get out of the corral, often erupting into violent bucking behavior. "You are not in Cuba City anymore, Mary," I would say. My hope was that eventually she would see that *no* was going to mean *no*, then she would stop charging the fence. It tried every bit of my patience.

Their new schools were huge. Bruce went from a town of 2000 to a school of 2000. Talk about culture shock. We were all experiencing it. I began to wonder if our family could make it in these new environs. I would come home from work dead tired and homesick. There I would meet my three lonely kids who were confused and homesick. Bruce seemed to be having trouble sleeping. I would get up to the bathroom at 4:00 A.M. and he would be watching television. We talked about it and he said he felt lost. He said the friends he had made were much different from his old friends.

I decided to seek counseling for all of us. I learned from the counselor that that the kids had lost their person to lean on … me. The mom they had always leaned on wanted to lean on someone herself. The kids had lost their support system and were acting out because of it. The counselor basically said I had to "buck-up" and fly right. My children needed to know that we were all going to be fine. I was their rock. I had to stop feeling sorry for myself and support them. Any tears I shed after that were shed in the shower as I got ready for work. Any misgivings I had, I kept to myself. It seemed to help. I began to lean on my spirituality, my faith. With the events of the separation and divorce, I had neglected my prayer life and church. Once I rekindled my faith, I began to feel stronger. I felt I could handle whatever might come my way. It was amazing to me what a difference this change made. *Why had I neglected it?*

Our rental house was often damaged by Mary. In a fit of anger Mary kicked a big hole in a wall. I bought *Readers' Digest Home Repair* book and Bruce and I set about repairing the damages. We became pretty adept at home repairs.

After moving to Arizona in November of 1980, we received word that Raul and Charlotte were getting married in the spring in Vegas, and they wanted to stop by Arizona afterward to see the kids. I invited them to stay at our house in Tempe. I told them I would go to Tucson to visit relatives for those few days and they could stay with the kids. They came and I left. It worked out for both of us.

My new friends at work teased me, "You mean your ex-husband and his new *wife* are coming to your house on their honeymoon?"

"Why not?" I replied, "The kids want to see them, and it will give me a chance to get away." The kids were excited about the visit, especially Mary. I thought it would ease their homesickness. There were too many separated couples trying to make their kids choose sides. Our kids had gone through enough of choosing up sides during our marriage. I liked Charlotte and I wanted the kids to like her. The kids said the visit went well.

I was having trouble spreading myself thin enough. Sometimes I felt like a chicken whose feathers had been plucked. The kids needed my support. My new job needed me. Mary's problems were escalating. Bruce was becoming a part of a school crowd that I did not like. I agreed that his new friends were nothing like his Cuba City friends. While they were friendly, somehow I did not trust them. In Cuba City Bruce had been a big fish in a little pond; now he was a little fish in a big pond and was not swimming well. As a freshman at McClintock High, he lost interest in sports. He went out for track but his allergies flared up. Football, basketball and track had been a big part of his life in Cuba City. I worried that he was getting lost in the shuffle.

One day near the end of his first school year in Tempe, Bruce became ill and had a high fever. I hated to leave him to go to work, but I had an important meeting and could not stay with him. About 10:00 A.M. I tried to call him and got no answer. I was worried, so I drove home. I found the garage open about two feet, and I could here music blasting from the house. *What is going on here?* I crouched down and went in through the opening in the garage and stepped into the house.

"What is going on here?" I yelled to be heard over the music. There were about a dozen kids who scattered like jelly beans when they saw me. They ran out the front and out the back. I went into the bedroom and found Bruce still in bed … and still with a high fever. "Bruce, what were you thinking? You know you can't have kids here when I'm at work?"

"I don't know, Mom. They came to the door and I couldn't just say 'go away,' so I let them in."

"Are they playing hooky?" I asked.

"I guess so," he replied.

I called the high school which was a half block away and said to the principal, "I just came home and found a dozen of your students in my house, obviously ditching school. Don't you keep track of them?"

"Mrs. Lagman, we have 2000 students and today 300 of them are absent. We cannot keep track of all of them." *You are not in Kansas anymore, Dorothy.*

I went into the bedroom and said to Bruce. "As soon as school is out, you are going back to Cuba City. This is not working for you. I will call your dad and tell him tonight." Bruce did not object, at least verbally. I hated to see him go. While he sometimes fought with Mary and Kim, at fifteen he was still the man of our house. I counted on him. Mary and Kim were twelve years old and needed after-school supervision. It was often late when I arrived home.

Bruce went back to Cuba City to live with Charlotte and Raul and Char's two kids. After a short time there, he called and begged me to let him come back to Arizona. He said, "Mom, could we move to another school? I don't know how to get out of that crowd. I don't think McClintock is working out for me." I missed him and was happy that he wanted to come back. I decided to try to buy a home in Mesa, near Westwood High. I had heard that it was a good school. Administration told me they had a system for checking on every student who was absent.

Since Raul and Char were living in our house in Cuba City, I asked Raul to buy me out of my interest. I became upset when he said he would give me $2500. We did not have an appraisal, but I was sure with the appreciation, I should at least receive ten or fifteen thousand. Again, I did not want to fight with him or turn the kids against him, so I took the $2500, and applied it to the down payment for my house in Mesa. In the divorce settlement I did not take any of his retirement (remember, my attorney said I could get half of it), I sold out cheap on the house, I didn't ask for alimony, and I could have asked for more support in the divorce … the price of peace was steep.

Our new home in Mesa was ten minutes from Friendship Village where I worked. We had a beautiful swimming pool and yard and the house was just right for us. It had three bedrooms, plus an addition which was going to be a guest bedroom. One problem with the addition was that you had to go out the back door and then into the addition through a sliding glass door. In the very back of the addition there was a state-of-the-art, cedar-lined sauna. Our new home had many unusual features like that. For instance, you had to open a kitchen cupboard to access the light switch. The previous owner was handy and had made many improvements; at least most of them were improvements.

Bruce, Mary, and Kim loved the pool with the slide. I especially liked the big stone fireplace in the family room. We spent many happy hours in the pool.

I was Catholic, a self-convert at age nineteen and had registered our family at Queen of Peace Church in Mesa. I enrolled Mary and Kim in the CCD (religion) classes. After a few months Mary was kicked out of the CCD classes because of her behavior. I was humiliated and a little perturbed. I had turned to my church thinking that it would be a good influence for my troubled daughter. I guess *she* was not good for *them*. I had never heard of a child getting kicked out of religion class. I found it depressing. I so wanted for her to be successful as a student and as a person. I thought spirituality might tame her a bit.

I was a spiritual person. I felt a close relationship with God. I talked to Him as my best friend. I knew He would see me through these trials with Mary. Every night I prayed for guidance. I prayed for her too and for all of us.

When I was a child Mom would often read the Bible to me. We would sing hymns together while she played the piano. I always felt peace during those times and remembered it always into adulthood. Even though Mom died shortly after my thirteenth birthday, she had filled me with pearls of wisdom which always came back to me, just when I needed it. Dad never attended church. When people asked him why he did not go to church with us, he would say, "My church is fishing out on the river." Mom and my friend Mary Frances' mother Fern were my role models for the kind of spiritual person and mother I wanted to be.

Why did I turn my back on God during those twenty years of marriage? Why, when I very much needed Him? Oh, I said my prayers and went to church, but it was such a superficial performance. I didn't feel it.

It wasn't long before son Mike completed high school and moved to Arizona with two of his friends. We were glad to see him. It was beginning to feel more like home for me. Shortly after that, Matt and his girlfriend Katy joined us in Arizona. Bruce was doing much better at Westwood and made the varsity football team. He was making some good friends, more like his Cuba City friends, I thought. Mary and Kim were attending school at Carson Jr. High next door to Westwood.

Our house was filled with much happiness on one hand and much strife on the other hand. My job was going well. I was promoted to the position of Village Administrator. I didn't receive a raise, just more responsibility. I was active in the Arizona State Nursing Home Association and was elected president. The strife came from home, contending with Mary and her increasingly bad behaviors. I was so busy with my job, the rearing of children, and the presidency of the association, that I began getting up at 4:00 A.M. to get a head start.

When I looked back on this time I was filled with guilt. *Those girls needed me and I was too wrapped up in my work to notice. If only I could go back to that point in time and start over.*

When Mary was in eighth grade at Carson Jr. High, I got a call that she was caught playing catch on the playground with a bag of marijuana. It was later proven that it was not marijuana … only parsley. It still gave me quite a scare. Mary was becoming well known to the SROs (School Resource Officers), policemen assigned to each school. Having a police officer at school was certainly a change for us. I could not imagine such a thing in Cuba City. The school counselor Mr. Ortega seemed to like Mary and worked hard to get her through the problems.

Mary was now dressing all in black with lots of eye make-up. She looked like pictures I had seen of Hell's Angels' motorcycle gangs. It made her furious if I criticized her dress or make up. There was no doubt that she enjoyed non-conforming. "I like the way I dress. If you don't like it, that's your problem," she would glare at me. She was becoming overweight.

Mary was suspended from school for two weeks for fighting with another girl. It was as if the hormones of adolescence were closing in on her and accelerating bad behavior. She could change from good to wild in a flash and for no apparent reason. Many times I would say, "What happened to put you in such a foul mood?"

"I'm always in a foul mood," she would answer. While I blamed adolescence for the increased emotional highs and lows, it was like nothing I had experienced with the boys. I still felt she was suffering from the early spoiling by her dad. I don't remember a single time of saying "no" to her that it did not send her into a tailspin. "No" or anything similar to "no" was her explosion button. I tried other words such as "not at this time," but it did not seem to make a difference. She wanted what she wanted and she wanted it now. I still held onto the idea that sooner or later she would learn that I would not change my mind and her behavior would improve.

Family events were almost always interrupted by a violent or hateful behavior episode acted out by Mary. Most of her anger seemed to be directed at me. She would often humiliate me in front of my brothers or sister by calling me names and belittling me. Sometimes I wondered why we even tried to attend family get-togethers. If we went to Tucson for a family picnic, she did the same thing. In looking back and trying to analyze what was going on with Mary at these events, I believe she felt unaccepted and felt she was an outsider … and behaved accordingly. She did not realize that her behavior was the reason for her not being an insider. I don't know what my brothers and sister thought, except I knew they were worried about me. "What are you going to do about her?" I was frequently asked. I pondered that question every night in bed. Sometimes I felt so angry at her it clouded my perspective.

One day I was cleaning the garage and Mary came out and said, "I need a new swimming suit."

"We could probably get you one next month," I said.

"I need it now!"

I told her, "We don't have the money right now, you will have to wait." She started calling me names and kicked a dust pile into my face. I chased her into the house where she grabbed hold of me, threw me down on the bed, and started beating on me. She was as strong as Charles Atlas when she blew. She got her hands around my neck and started choking me. I could not get out of the hold.

Son Mike came in, saw what was happening, and grabbed her and threw her down on the floor, holding her there until she promised to stop. Mike was the biggest of the boys and in good shape. Even Mike had trouble restraining her. *What if Mike had not been there? Would she have killed me? I don't know. Was my demise going to be the next cause for her Black Puppy Syndrome?* I trembled at the thought. Mike was very upset.

Mary was still furious at me. When I finished the garage I went for a swim. She came out, picked up the big picnic bench, and threw it at me while I was in the water. Thank God she missed.

These two back-to-back events left me weak and shaken. I locked myself in my bathroom, collapsing onto the floor, grabbing my knees and sobbing. *My God, my God, why have You forsaken me? What did I do to deserve this? Will it ever end?* I sat there on the floor, unable to stop crying. I felt helpless and hopeless. I was a solution-minded person and yet I could not figure out the answer. I knew that God answered prayers, but I had been praying about this for a long, long time. I often asked the Blessed Virgin Mary to pray for me. I figured she understood motherhood. I looked down and saw a large, tear-drop-shape of blood on my wrist, near the palm of my hand. It was weird. It was not an ordinary drop of blood. At first I thought I had been injured in the pool. I examined myself and could find no scratch or wound. *How did it get there? Was it some sort of message? Was God trying to tell me that he had not forsaken me?*

Whatever it was, it jolted me into pulling myself together. Somehow I felt blessed. This was a moment in time that would return to me often in the coming years when I needed an extra dose of faith … and I would find comfort in it. For awhile I questioned it. Then I decided that this was something to accept and not question. Years later I read that The Blessed Virgin Mary had shed tears of blood on several occasions. *That's what it was on my hand. The Blessed Mother had shed a tear of blood to let me know that she was watching over me.* From then on I had a special devotion to her.

11

From Bad to Worse

Following the gasoline incident in chapter two where she nearly blew us all away and was arrested, Mary had an idea which she thought would make things better for her. She seemed to be striking out in Arizona. School was going south. She was not succeeding at home. She decided that she should move back to Wisconsin with her dad Raul and his new wife Char and Char's two children. I had mixed feelings about her going back to Wisconsin. Part of me thought it was a useless idea and would not work. The other part of me felt that we could use some time out from the chaos. I called Raul to discuss it. "Raul, she wants to come there and I have almost reached the end of my rope." He was hesitant. I had kept him informed about most of the Arizona happenings.

Since he spoiled her rotten, he should have a taste of parenting her. I guess I felt that at least he should suffer some of the results. I knew in my heart that this change would not work for any of them. Raul did not have the time, energy, patience, or concentration. He had a new wife and a new life. Mary insisted upon it. I knew she was counting on it to solve her problems. It was worth a try. Anyway, I was fresh out of ideas. So Mary went there and enrolled in school in Cuba City.

For us … Bruce, Kim and me, it was a peace we had never experienced. Bruce was busy with his school activities and athletics. Kim turned into my little homemaker. She cooked and cleaned. Bruce and Kim got along fine. Of course, Bruce was a typical adolescent and capable of his own shenanigans from time to time, but nothing out of the ordinary like there used to be with Mary. I found that I expected more from him. It was as if all my patience had been used up on Mary. I was glad I now had more time give them. In my lifetime so far I had not appreciated the heavenly feeling of peace. It made me feel giddy sometimes.

My job was going well. I was quite proud of my accomplishments. I found that I had a talent for building strong teams of employees. I felt I brought fun to the workplace. I always dressed up for Halloween and enjoyed our work parties. I valued all the employees and residents. It did not matter to me if an employee was the dishwasher or a department head. I valued them and I liked them. And, of course, I loved our residents.

Our peace at home was short-lived. A couple of months after Mary went to Wisconsin, I began receiving phone calls from Raul. "She won't listen to me," he would say. "She won't mind me. It's not working out."

I wanted to say, "It's about time you experienced what I have been going through." But I didn't. I would listen to him. He would ask for advice. I didn't have any. All I said was, "I know what you mean. It's tough. I have been there."

I was, I'm sorry to say, only too glad to pass the buck. I must confess that I took a sick pleasure in seeing him harvest the fruits of his labor, or at least to have him share the agony.

One evening the phone rang. It was Raul. "Mary has run away. There are two boys also missing. The police think they stole a Chevy Blazer." I did not want to hear this. I was reluctant to break the calm that we were experiencing. Not now, God. Please not now.

I could not imagine that these kids would get very far. She was still only fourteen and I think the other boys were also fourteen. In about forty-eight hours I got another call. They had been apprehended near Ogallala, Nebraska … almost into Colorado. They were all okay, although it appeared, I was told, as if they had gone into a ditch with the Blazer. It also appeared that they were headed for Arizona. Raul called me after they were apprehended. They had been put in jail in Ogallala. "What should I do? He asked.

"Raul, I have to leave it up to you. This happened on your watch." I was reluctant to be involved. He had lots more money than I did, and I was only too happy to let him handle it. When things happened on my turf, I handled them. Raul and the other parents chartered a small plane to Nebraska and brought the kids back to the Grant County, Wisconsin jail. I guess they were let out on bail.

Mary's disposition hearing was coming up, and Raul wanted me there for it. Since Steve, our oldest son, was getting married in Wisconsin in May, we arranged for the hearing to be scheduled while I was in Wisconsin for the wedding. When we arrived in Wisconsin, it seemed to me that Mary's behavior was worse. She seemed extra mad at me and refused to relate to anyone in a positive way. I took her to Dubuque to buy something to wear for the wedding, but the trip was a disaster. We finally got her outfitted in something, although I did not feel it was appropriate for a wedding.

The wedding was beautiful and all went well. It was good to see my old friends. Mary managed to get into some liquor and got drunk at the reception.

By this time I was pretty sure she had been a fetal alcohol baby, so when she drank, her drinking went out of control. Her brothers got her out of the reception without ruining the day.

On Monday we met with the official at the Grant County Court regarding what was going to happen to Mary. "After disposition is Mary going to be living with her father in Cuba City?" he asked.

"Well, you see, sir," Raul fumbled, "We can't have her here. You see, I have a new wife and she has two younger children. We can't handle her. We won't be able to take her."

I looked over at Mary. Her face fell and she looked down. I thought I could read her mind. "No one wants me," is what I read on her face.

In an instant I made up my mind. "I want her to come back to Arizona with me," I stated firmly, without looking at Raul. It seemed to me he only cared about his new life and family. It didn't matter to him that he had a huge part in enhancing Mary's problems. It did not matter to him that we in Arizona had been through hell? Now he just wanted her to go away. When I reflected on the many difficulties between Raul and me, that moment was the one that stands out as the most difficult for me to swallow. She was our child, and as troublesome as it could be, there was no doubt in my mind that I loved her and wanted her. I could not imagine any child thinking they were not wanted.

And so it was decided … I would take Mary back to Arizona to live with us. It still did not occur to me that Mary might be suffering from mental illness, nor was it ever suggested at that time by any of the counseling we sought. Was my vision impaired by the chaos around me? When I look back I wonder why I did not decide on my own that Mary was mentally ill. After all, I had a degree in psychology and I was a nurse. I guess I could not see the forest for the trees.

Again, I remind you that Mary had many admirable qualities. If she were your friend she would stand up for you, regardless of the fact that it may get her into trouble. Many of the problems she experienced, especially after high school, were because she was trying to help a friend. She could also be lots of fun and on those occasions she seemed so good you almost forget the bad times. If only we could channel her strong will into positive undertakings, she would excel. I believed that.

The good times gave me hope that she would eventually get it together. And I prayed. And prayed. It was the glue that held me together.

By her sophomore year in high school, Mary had put on more weight, still wore lots of make-up, and would still only wear black clothes. She looked like a biker without a bike. Some of her friends were spooky. I would ask her, "Is that girl on drugs?"

Of course the answer was always, "No, that's a stupid question." It was interesting that she seemed to have friends whom I would term weird, but she also had friends whom I would have chosen for her … normal kids. I guessed she was trying to establish her identity, to figure out who the heck she was. Her weird friends seemed to like me. Mary would say, "My friends like you, I don't know why."

Our everyday relationship was difficult. If Mary accompanied us out to dinner, she made a scene. She either became upset at the waiter or at me. She also had no regard for my budget, ordering gobs of food and always dessert. I found myself letting her, so she would not make a scene; perhaps taking the way of least resistance. I don't know why I continued to take her out to eat except that I was an eternal optimist. I thought each time was going to be better. You know the story about the little optimist who thought if there was a pile of manure there had to be a pony nearby? That was I.

My responsibilities at Friendship Village were increasing. Thank God I loved my work. I felt successful as a leader of the Village and in the senior retirement industry. I was on the Board of the state association and felt I was a vital part of what was happening in the industry. Again, I had two separate and distinct lives. I had many good friends. My closest friends were aware of the storm within our household, and many of them had witnessed it close-up. During those days I never knew what I would find when I arrived home. Would I see a police car? Would there be a fight going on with Mary and Bruce? I could almost depend upon some sort of challenge awaiting me.

During Mary's sophomore year I had to attend a three-day association meeting in Tucson, a hundred miles away. My son Matt and girlfriend Katy were going to stay with Mary, Bruce and Kim. Our meeting was at a hotel and I was rooming with my friend Fran. Our second day there Fran had gone down to a breakfast meeting and I was in the room. Fran came back upstairs and said to me, "Gayle, there is some kind of emergency at your home, and they are trying to get hold of you."

I called home. I cannot even remember to whom I spoke: "Mary has stabbed Bruce. He has gone to the hospital and Mary has run out of the house," they said.

"How serious is it?" I asked with my heart in my throat.

"We don't know. She stabbed him in the back with a paring knife."

"What hospital?"

"Tempe St. Lukes."

"What happened?"

"All I know is that Bruce and Mary got into it over the car keys."

"Oh, my God. My God," was all I could say. What a horrible thing.

I said a silent prayer for Bruce. I was also thinking: *Mary absolutely needs more help than I can give her. For sure she needs to be hospitalized. They better think this is acute enough for admission. Somehow I have to make it happen.*

I was in no shape to drive back to Mesa, so my sister-in-law Iris who lived in Tucson, drove me back. I prayed hard that day. I learned what constant prayer meant. We went straight to the hospital, where I learned that Bruce was going to be okay. Mary had just missed his kidney, the doctor explained. They would keep him for a few days to make sure he did not get an infection. *Another narrow escape. Thank you God.* I usually hold up pretty well during an emergency, and then when it is over I collapse in a heap. And that I did.

Mary was found and arrested shortly. I got on the phone to some people I knew and they put me in touch with the adolescent unit at Camelback Hospital … a psych hospital. I begged the admission person to find a bed for her. She said, "We are full, but we may have an opening soon. Let me work on it."

I felt so strongly that another stint in juvenile hall or prison would just make Mary worse and was not what she needed. She needed intensive psychiatric help. We got an opening at Camelback, and I had to persuade the courts that she needed this treatment. They finally concurred, and Mary was taken to Camelback. She was not to have any family visits for three weeks. Even though I did not visit her, I became immediately involved with the family group, which met on Tuesday evenings, without the presence of the patients.

The hospital was about twenty miles from our home. In addition to family night, Mary and I went to individual family counseling with a psychologist every Thursday evening. After the three weeks I was allowed to visit her. After one month, I was allowed to bring her home on the weekend for a day visit—no overnights at that point.

I learned a lot from the family group sessions. At one family session a new woman joined our group. I could see by her demeanor that she was very angry. When our facilitator asked her if she would like to share anything, she said, "I brought my teen-age daughter here today. I am so angry at her and at my husband. He has spoiled her rotten. She runs all over me and he gives her everything," she spouted.

Wow, that could be me. I felt the same way. Was that how my anger at Mary and Raul looked? I'm afraid it was. Even now when I look back, I realize that I had been angry for a very long part of my life over the situation with Mary and Raul;

the spoiling of Mary Frances. And that is not the only reason. I was angry at Raul because I felt he made it impossible for me to be Mary's nurturing mother. I always had to be the bad guy. Someone had to try to control her, didn't they?

On Saturday, while bringing Mary home for a visit, I related to Mary about the new mom in our group. "You know Mary, there was a woman who brought her daughter into Camelback on Tuesday and I saw myself in her."

"What do you mean?" she asked.

"She was so angry at her husband and daughter. She said her husband spoiled her daughter rotten. I saw myself. I was angry at Raul and you. Could you see it?"

"I didn't know you were angry. I thought you hated me."

I sat in stunned silence for a moment. "Oh, no, honey, I never hated you. I was angry at a situation that I could not change. I could see damage being done and I could not stop it. The only thing I could do was be angry, I guess. But I did not realize I was angry until last night, when I heard this other mother."

That was a revelation for both of us. The realization that because he spoiled Mary so fervently that it took away my ability to be close to her, was a major insight for me. I could see then that I had taken the role of the one who tried to make her mind. If he would not do it, then I felt I had to; thus, in Mary's mind Raul was the good parent and I was the bad one. Or put another way, she felt he loved her and felt I hated her. Participating in that family group for almost a year was therapeutic for me. I was able to see my contributions to Mary's behavior. It was a bitter pill to swallow, but necessary. I had helped to perpetuate some of the untoward behaviors.

The individual sessions with Mary were lead by a psychiatrist, Dr. Stanton. He was a short, mature man who wore glasses, had a kind face, and had a good sense of humor. He was not like some of the psychiatrists I had met, who looked and acted as if they needed a psychiatrist. I liked him and I think Mary did too. I saw that Mary tried to manipulate him by distracting him with stuff that was not relevant to what we were discussing. Usually he caught onto her.

At one of our sessions Dr. Stanton noticed that Mary was kicking at my foot while we were sitting there in his office. He said, "I notice that Mary is kicking at you."

"Yes," I said, "She frequently does that."

"Do you have any idea why she does that?" He asked.

"To irritate me," I offered.

"How about you, Mary? Any ideas why you do that to your mother?"

"No." she answered.

"Well, I think that is Mary's way of showing affection to you. It is the equivalent of a hug. She is not comfortable hugging you, so she expresses herself by kicking at you," he offered. "What do you think of that suggestion, Mary?"

"It sounds kind of silly," Mary ventured.

"People do some silly things when they are not comfortable showing their feelings, huh!" Dr. Stanton said. "Mom, what do you think?" he frequently called me "Mom" as if he were Mary calling me "Mom."

"I've always found it annoying, because I thought she was trying to annoy me. Maybe if I think of it as a hug, I won't find it annoying, but I would still rather have a hug," I said.

Another revelation, which Dr. Stanton revealed to me in front of Mary after a few months into therapy, "Gayle, do you realize that Mary is governed by two very opposing strong emotions? One is a mortal fear that something will happen to you. The opposing one is that she wants something to happen to you and is hell-bent on causing something to happen to you."

"That is a scary thought," I said. "They seem mutually exclusive. How could she have them both?"

"It is strange, but they are behind a lot of her behavior toward you." He said.

"Is that true, Mary?" I asked.

"If he says it's true, it must be," not admitting it outright.

"So, am I to understand that if she made something happen to me, then her other fear that something might happen to me would be realized? (I thought of the Black Puppy Syndrome.) How do I handle this?"

"That is what we will be working on." Dr. Stanton explained.

I pondered this information over and over in the months and years afterward. It seemed to me that these opposing thoughts did not make sense. Was that what they called a "love/hate" relationship?

One day on our return trip to the hospital, Mary said, "Mom, I need to stop at the drug store to buy some purple hair dye."

"What for?" I asked

"To dye my hair. What else would you use dye for?" she said.

"If you are going to buy purple dye, you will have to buy two of them, so I can have one."

"Why would you need one?"

"Because, if you dye your hair purple, I will dye my hair purple." I said.

"No way. Why would you dye your hair purple? You would look stupid."

"No more stupid than you would look."

"Forget it!" she said.

Another unforgettable time on the drive back to the hospital: She had become upset at home. She said she did not want to help decorate the Christmas tree at home, but neither did she want us to decorate it without her. Many times it was a problem to get her to commit. Did she want to stay or go? Did she want to decorate or not? As we were driving down Scottsdale Road about fifteen minutes from the hospital she began pummeling me in the face and all over my upper body. Like a dummy, I kept driving. It was a wonder I did not have an accident. We were just minutes away from the hospital. Something told me to keep going and get there as fast as I could. When we arrived, she got out of the car and went in. I waited a few minutes to try and get control of myself then I went into the hospital. I fell apart. I was sobbing as I related to the nurse what had happened. I was beaten and bruised on the outside and on the inside. Mary's week-ends at home were cancelled. She did not even get to come home for Christmas that year.

If it sounds like we lived crisis to crisis; I guess we did. Because Mary was in the hospital and we were all learning, I felt hopeful that in the new year things were going to get better.

On another infamous drive back to the hospital, we were driving on Pima Rd. which was like a highway, with speeds of 55 miles per hour. Mary was furious about something and an argument ensued.

"I'm getting out of this car!" she yelled and opened the door.

"Stay in the car," I yelled as I put on the brakes and pulled over.

"You bitch," she shouted. "You will never see me again." She jumped out of the car before it came to a complete stop.

There was a semi-truck coming from the opposite direction. She began walking slowly and deliberately across the highway. The semi could see what she was doing and began to brake and honk the horn. I hid my head on the steering wheel and prayed. *Oh, God, don't let it end like this.* I could not look. I was sure that she was going to be hit by the semi. It seemed like forever, and then I heard the semi start up again. I pulled my head up and could see Mary standing on the other side of the road. Through my tears I could see her look at me defiantly. I had to sit there for another fifteen minutes before I could drive. She did not say anything for the rest of the trip and I couldn't. I had the feeling that she was as shaken as I was. It was one of the many times she flirted with death, with me as the audience.

Faith was my constant companion in those days. I literally prayed constantly. Little prayers, *God help me, give me strength for the journey.* Every time I arrived at the hospital, which was built in the shadow of Camelback Mountain, I would look up at the mountain and say part of the 121st Psalm: *I will lift up mine eyes unto the hills from whence cometh my help. My help cometh from the Lord, who made Heaven and Earth.* I could not count the number of times I prayed that Psalm. Those prayers and my faith saved my sanity. God brought Mary to me through adoption for a reason, and I knew it was not for the reason of giving up on her.

One Sunday in church the message was about how God could always see the good in people. The priest said that pursuing the good in people can make them good. I was faithful in my pursuit of the good in Mary. I knew it was there.

Many times through the years, a friend would say to me, "If my kid ever did that I would kick them out and never see them again."

"That is conditional love," I would tell them. "You say you will only love them if they live up to your expectations. I say, "I will love you forever, no matter what." Not to be confused with, "I love those terrible things you do."

I also learned that what people think they will do when faced with a troublesome kid, and what they actually do, are distant cousins. The tie that binds us with our kids is an unbreakable golden cord … a replacement for the umbilical cord that tied us to them en utero.

Toward the end of Mary's hospitalization, she developed a wonderful idea about helping other kids. She was going to call it "Straight Talk from Teens." One of the female therapists, Chris, at the hospital was encouraging her and helping her with it. The idea was for Mary and other kids who had been in trouble to help teens make better decisions than Mary and friends had made, and to show them how miserable it was to get on the wrong side of the law. Mary worked hard on it. She was excited. I saw something in her that I had not seen before: She was feeling successful and feeling good about herself. I told her that I was proud of her.

I attended Mary's first presentation at Arizona State University. There were lots of kids there and she did a great job. This was the first time I remember feeling proud of her since she was very young. This program was making her feel like she was making a difference in young people's lives. She was getting lots of positive attention for the first time. Her photo was in all the local papers. I thought my prayers had been answered.

Mary was discharged from the hospital, but we attended AfterCare once a week for the next year. We still had our difficulties but I was more hopeful about her success than I had ever been. When I pressed Dr. Stanton for a diagnosis of Mary's mental problems, I was told that she was having a Developmental Adjustment Reaction. When they explained it to me, it sounded like she was "stuck in the mud" and unable to grow up. It sounded pretty vague to me. I was hoping for something that would require some medication which would bring her back to normal. By the way, I found that psychiatrists and their cohorts do not like the word "normal." I think it is because in their world there is no such thing as "normal," which is defined in my dictionary as being "free from physical or mental disorder." Maybe they do not believe anyone is normal in the most literal sense of the word?

For Mary's "Straight-Talk" program she was nominated by the governor of Arizona for a national youth award and won. She was to go to California to receive the award from the Secretary of Education. She could take one other person with her. I thought sure she would take me, but she chose to take Chris, the therapist, with her. I felt a little hurt, but I understood, since Chris had helped her develop the program.

Mary went to California as planned. I expected that she would be very excited and happy when she returned. I could not wait to hear about the award ceremony. When she came back, she was visibly upset. She seemed both depressed and short-tempered. She said she did not want to talk about it. I felt something had happened on the trip, but she would not say anything to me about it, and became angry when I asked.

Months later I found out that Chris had molested her in the hotel room. Her therapist had molested her. The details were never revealed to me. She did not want anything more to do with Chris or the Straight Talk program. She was clearly disillusioned. I wanted to press charges but Mary insisted I stay out of it. She said she would deny that it happened if I got involved.

I tried to convince her that she did not need Chris to do the program. She just clammed up. When I look back, I cannot believe that I did not take action against the hospital in spite of Mary's feelings. Mary was a minor, manipulated and molested by her therapist. The therapist lost her job for reasons not divulged to us. Mary reported the molestation to Camelback Hospital, at least to her doctor. (Mary discusses this in her chapters of this book). The way it was presented to me was that the therapist attempted to molest her. Later it was related that she was molested.

In December of 1984 we had just returned from Christmas shopping. We were excited because all the boys were going to be home for Christmas. The phone rang and I answered in the kitchen. Bruce evidently had picked up the phone in the bedroom. It was my neighbor and friend from Cuba City, Joan Bainbridge. "Gayle, I'm afraid I have some bad news. Raul had a heart attack at home and we could not save him. We did everything possible. There were several doctors there, in addition to the rescue squad and support from Madison."

Bruce came running into the kitchen having heard on the bedroom phone what happened. He was crying. Mary heard him and came running, demanding to know what had happened. "Mary, your dad had a heart attack and they could not save him. I'm afraid he's gone." She ran screaming at the top of her lungs around the house, shouting, "Tell me that's not true. Tell me he didn't die. Please, Mom, tell me it didn't happen." Kim didn't know what to do. She stayed close to me and looked very sad too. I have no idea what she really felt. This dad of hers had never given her his love. She tried in her little ways to comfort everyone.

My friend Joan further related, "Raul had made rounds at the hospital and came home feeling fine. After he went to bed Char noticed strange breathing noises, and tried to wake him. When she couldn't, she called for emergency help. Our neighbor, who was an EMT, was there in no time," Joan related.

Just two weeks before his death, our son Steve, the pre-med student, had called me and said, "Mom, I am worried about Dad. He eats all the wrong things, he doesn't exercise, he forgets to take his blood pressure medicine, and he has the family history. He has the perfect coronary profile. I have tried to talk to him about it, but he doesn't seem to listen." I had tried many times to get Raul to take better care of himself. I did not love him, but I cared about him. He was the father of our six children. I had spent twenty years of my life with him. Now I hurt for all of them.

12

Back to the Drawing Board

The kids insisted that I accompany them to the funeral in Wisconsin. It was the week before Christmas. Getting tickets on December 19 was difficult. I didn't have the cash, so put our tickets on a credit card, $2500 dollars worth. We had to provide proof of the death and had to fly through Las Vegas to Des Moines, Iowa, where friends would pick us up and drive us the 250 miles to Cuba City. When we landed, the weather was awful: rain, sleet, snow and wind, and cold. I had forgotten how cold Wisconsin could be. The roads were slick and I was a nervous wreck by the time we arrived. Thank God we had an excellent driver.

It was a sad time. Thankfully, I was filled with memories of happier times, not the memories of the tough times. I remembered how Raul used to love the "I Love Lucy" shows. He would literally roll on the floor laughing. He loved sports. It amazed me at how hooked on sports Raul was, when many of them he never saw until he arrived in the states in 1958.

I remembered how we teased him about his English. He often got our sayings mixed up. He would say, "Don't cross your bridges before your eggs are hatched." Or, "That woman has a peach ice cream complexion." In the Philippines the letter "p" is sounded like an "f" and the short "a" sound is pronounced like our short "u" sound. He would ask for a rag and I would think he wanted a rug. When he first moved to the states, he was mortified that there was a football team called the Green Bay Packers. It sounded like the "F" word to him. We also got a kick out of him when he said we were going to a "farty." He was always good-natured about our teasing.

I remembered the time I drove to Dubuque to have my eyes checked. When I got back to my car in the parking garage, my battery was dead. I called Raul and he loaded up the kids and came over to Dubuque. He drove into the garage and I got in with him and drove out with him in his car. He said to the woman at the garage pay center, "Our car is up there with a dead battery in it."

The woman began screaming, "A dead body. Oh my God, this has never happened to me before!" It took me a minute to realize how she could possibly think there was a dead body up there. It was the way Raul pronounced "battery!" Mary got such a laugh out of that. I also remembered how much I loved Raul before it turned sour.

My heart ached for the kids. This was the first major loss in their lives. The scene of those kids surrounding the casket with their arms around each other will stay with me forever. *Raul, we made some awfully good kids together; I am so sorry that you could not have lived to see them grown and to see your grandchildren."*

The service was meaningful and full of townspeople. My close friend Peg came from Fort Atkinson. Father Kurz came from Argyle, Wisconsin, to do the service. He had been our priest in Fort Atkinson and Raul was very fond of him.

Charlotte invited me and all the kids to sit with her and her two children in the front row. Father Kurz opened the service by saying, "Charlotte, Gayle, and all the kids ..." I was reasonably sure that the people in Cuba City had not witnessed a funeral where the first and second wife and all the kids were sitting harmoniously together in the front row. It made me glad that the fourth of July before his death, Raul, Char, and the kids came to Mesa, got a motel nearby, and spent lots of time with us. On the Fourth, I made Filipino food and all the kids swam in our pool. It was a nice family get-together ... even Mary had seemed to enjoy it. I thanked God that both Charlotte and I were the kind of people that could do this for the kids. A death is hard enough without kids having to be pulled between two parents. For that matter, life is hard enough without kids having to be involved in a tug-of-war between parents.

After the funeral was over we headed back to Arizona, arriving two days before Christmas. Steve arrived on Christmas Eve, and we had a very necessary healing and closeness that Christmas. Death had made our family realize how much we meant to each other and how quickly our lives could change.

It was back to the drawing board with Mary. She had been so close to exiting her cocoon with her Straight Talk program, and then the episode with Chris pushed her back. Then Raul died ... was she going to be in her cocoon forever? I did not recognize the depression in Mary. I knew she was grieving, and it was difficult to comfort her. Every emotion she felt seemed to spew from her in anger. She did not cry and throw her arms around me, except on very rare occasions. She experienced more fighting and strife at school.

The residents and staff at Friendship Village were wonderful to me during this time. They sent me cards with words of love and support. I truly appreciated them and still enjoyed my job there. What joy there was in loving your work.

Working there was like living in my hometown Wray. They were salt-of-the-earth people. The same year that Raul died, my boss, the Executive Director resigned. I was in line for the position, but was informed by Mike, the regional director, that they were going to bring in a "seasoned" person from their ranks to take the job. "We value you highly," he explained, "but Friendship Village is our largest client and requires someone with vast experience."

"But, Mike," I said to him. "I have been here four years. I know this place. I have the respect of the staff and the residents and the Board of Directors. Is it because I'm a woman?"

"No, not at all," he assured me.

I decided right then and there that if I was not going to get the Executive Director position, I was going to look for another position with which I could grow.

"I do appreciate your honesty with me, Mike. Now I realize that I must look for a position elsewhere." I was honest with him.

"Now, Gayle, do not do anything foolish. You are valuable to our organization."

"Mike, I have to think about my family and my future."

"Gayle, at least give me until next Tuesday before you do anything, and I will get back to you," he said.

"Okay," I agreed. In the meantime, I put some feelers out for a new opportunity. I felt disappointed that the management company did not seem to appreciate my talents.

The next Tuesday I met with Mike and he said, "Congratulations, Gayle, you are the new Executive Director of Friendship Village."

I was surprised and thrilled. I knew I could do it. I don't know how much Mike knew about my "home" challenges, but I couldn't help wondering if he was afraid those challenges would interfere with my job. I was determined to keep my home life separate and distinct from my life at work, and I thought I did a pretty good job of that.

At any rate, I began my new position with a great team of people and the support of most of the residents. I did have a couple of men residents and one woman resident who came to see me and said, "We like you and you are a nice person, but this is no job for a woman. It takes a man for this big operation."

I said to them. "All I ask is that you keep an open mind and give me a chance. If, after a year you feel the same way, I want you to come back and tell me." Not one person came back except to tell me they had been wrong. They became my biggest supporters! It was a consuming job. There were so many challenges, but we met them one by one. I was always honest with the residents and staff. Previous administrations had been tight with the information given to residents. I gave them the info they wanted. I felt that honesty would lead to trust, and if they could come to trust me, it would be more than half the battle. It was.

Our family life went bumpily along. Bruce was graduated from Westwood and eventually went out on his own … with a little coaxing. If only I could get Kim and Mary graduated and out on their own I may find a life for myself. I had heard about the "empty nest syndrome," and did not feel I would suffer from that malady.

Freedom was not to be. One day I arrived home to find a lengthy letter from Mary. Basically, it was a good-bye letter. A suicide letter. She indicated that she had reached the end of the line. She apologized for causing so much trouble and said she loved us. She said not to waste our time trying to find her.

I immediately called Dr. Stanton at the hospital and read the letter to him. He felt we should notify the authorities to help find her. He reminded me, "Mary is not only capable of making threats, but she is capable of carrying them out."

"That's why I am afraid," I remembered that from our sessions.

"Gayle, we also need to talk about what to do when we find her," he said.

"What are you thinking?" I asked.

"You know she has had the best psych care our area has to offer," he said.

"Why don't we let her see how the other half lives?"

"How do we do that?" I asked.

"We need to have her committed to the County Crisis Unit. We could hold her there for at least three days while they assess her danger to herself. It may be an eye-opener for her," he offered. "A sort of a shock treatment."

"I'm in favor of anything that might help." I said.

I had a bad feeling about this threat. Mary had made many threats, but this one seemed different. Lately I had been having deepened feelings of hopelessness about our situation with Mary. We were living from one crisis to another. I seemed to be running out of steam; maybe Mary was running out of steam too.

Mary often said she was going to kill herself, but Dr. Stanton and I felt those other threats were mostly attention-getters. This time she left a detailed letter and we all felt it could be real. I prayed hard that they would find her before she tried anything stupid. Again my prayers were answered.

The police located Mary after several hours, with help from her friends. I had communicated to the police that when they found her she was to be committed to the County Crisis Center. I met them there and signed the papers.

I didn't know how other county crisis centers operated, or how they would appear to someone going there for the first time, but I was surprised. Maybe shocked was a better word. This was truly the other side of the coin from Camelback Hospital. There were men and women mixed in together. Young people and old people were all thrown into one huge ward.

It was chaotic. There was an old fellow walking around in circles over and over again. Then someone hollered "Fred!" and he would change directions and walk the circle the other way. This was constant. One evening when I was there the nurse said, "Fred, I have your bus ticket." Fred went up, got his bus ticket, and went out the door. I was shocked to think that Fred was being released. I saw several situations like that in the week that Mary was there. I could believe that Arizona was number fifty in the list of states on money spent for mental health.

If seeing "how the other half lived" was going to help Mary, they chose the right place. I thought about how I would feel if committed to that place. I would be scared to death and I could not help but worry about Mary. While she had lots of problems, it looked to me as if she were the most mentally sound person there. Many of them seemed not to be living in reality. Of course, Mary was scared to death too, and begged me to get her out of there. I went there every evening to see her.

Did you ever have a week that did you in? I had mine. The social worker at the hospital informed me on Tuesday that Mary was pregnant. They automatically did pregnancy tests on all admissions. I was in a state of shock. I must have driven home, but afterward, I did not remember driving there. I sat in the car for a long time, my mind in a muddle. *What now? How much more?*

God, where are you? I need You to find me and hold me together. I cannot handle this by myself. I did not tell anyone in the family that day. I couldn't bring myself to talk about it. I lay awake the whole night until the alarm went off.

I was on automatic pilot at work that day. On Wednesday evening, my daughter Kim came to me and confided that she too was pregnant. She said that she and Eric planned to get married. "Kim, you are seventeen years old. You are a senior in high school. You haven't finished high school. Eric hasn't either. What do either one of you know about marriage or children? How will you support them?" They did not have the answers. I certainly did not have the answers. My mind was still reeling from the news of Mary's pregnancy … and now two of them. I could not think straight.

God, I do not believe in abortion, but I do not believe in children being born to mothers who are still children themselves or children who cannot emotionally be a mother. What is the right thing?

What were my options here? Both girls would be eighteen before their babies were born. I would have no legal say in what they were going to do anyway!

I needed support. I looked in the church bulletin and found that there was a prayer meeting at Queen of Peace that night at 7:00 P.M.. I dragged myself there. I had never been to a prayer meeting before. It turned out that it was a charismatic prayer meeting. There were about a dozen very nice people there. There was a man leading the meeting. He seemed to know that I was in crisis. As he led me to a chair in the circle, he said, "You are having problems with your daughters."

"How did you know?" I bawled. They prayed over me. They prayed for Mary and Kim. I felt a calm come over me.

Afterward, there was a very nice woman named Anita who came over to me. She put her hand on my shoulder, looked me in the eye, and said, "Honey, I know how angry and upset you are about your daughters, but I can tell you one thing for sure, love is the answer."

I thanked her. If only it were that simple. I went to my car. As I drove up the street, there was a Travelodge on the corner. There was a marquis out front with a saying on it. I always read it when I went to church. Tonight it said, "Love is the Answer." I said, "Okay, God, I got the message." Guess I needed a whack on the head! I felt comforted. I found out later that Anita died that same month. She had breast cancer. I only met her that one time, but I felt strangely close to her. I was sure that she was an angel sent to me by God. *Thank you, Anita.* In my head I went from feeling hopeless to feeling positive that we would get through it. *Take a day at a time.*

Kim went ahead with her plans to get married. I tried to tell her that pregnancy was not a good reason to get married. She transferred to a special high school where she took child care classes. Mary also went there. Mary had decided to give her baby up for adoption. She was now experiencing the hormonal roller coaster of pregnancy, which only enhanced her sunny disposition. She brought home ultra sound photos … it was going to be a boy. She showed them to everyone. I was getting worried that she may change her mind about the adoption.

In September, before she was going to be eighteen in October, Mary got a jail sentence. According to the authorities, she would be held until she was eighteen and then they would let her go. When she came home after jail, she announced that a social worker had told her, "Don't let anyone tell you that you have to give your baby up for adoption. It is your decision."

"So, I want you to know that I am keeping my baby," she informed me.

"And you are going to raise it and care for it and love it and support it, right?"

"Right."

"How?" I asked.

"I'll figure it out."

"Mary, I am not raising your baby. I can't. I am worn out. I have a very demanding job. Babies take lots of care."

"You won't have to do anything," she promised.

I knew in my heart that I was going to be raising a child. I prayed. *God, give me strength for this journey."* I used to wonder if God got tired of all my requests. I wondered if any day He might say, "Enough, already."

I had no time to think about what it would mean to be a grandma. I really had disassociated myself from thinking of this impending birth as anything but a job I was not going to be able to do. All I could think of were the questions. *How? How am I going to do this? Where is this going? How can I nurture another child?*

When Mary went into labor, I went with her to the hospital. She did not handle pain very well. She demanded pain relief. After hours and hours of labor, they did an X-Ray and told me they were going to have to do a cesarean section … she could not have a normal delivery. They said I could don surgical clothes and be in the operating room with her.

I was totally unprepared for the birth of my first grandchild. When I laid eyes on him, it was the first time I had realization that he was my first grandchild. He was a tiny, beautiful baby, a gift from God. When they handed him to me, the tears were running down my face under the surgical mask. I loved him instantly and vowed at that moment, that whatever it took, I would be there for him.

She named him Andrew Mariano (the Mariano was Raul's middle name, which was the maiden name of his mother). Mary was very much the proud mother while she was in the hospital. Andrew was not only my first grandchild; he was the first nephew for Kim and the boys. They all seemed thrilled with him. Kim and Bruce were still living at home. Mike lived nearby. Matt and Katy were still around. Andrew drew lots of attention.

I think Mary really tried to be a mother. I could tell she loved Andrew. She liked to dress him up and show him off to her friends. When it came to getting up in the middle of the night, she just couldn't do it, it seemed. I would let him cry as long as I dared in the hope that she would get up and feed him. One night, I she yelled, "Shut that kid up, or I'll shut him up!" From then on I did the night feedings. Thank God he was a good baby and started sleeping through the night by six weeks. Kim became Andrew's baby sitter during the day. She bathed him and mostly took care of him. Mary did not seem comfortable with the newborn stuff.

"Maybe when he gets a little older, she will take hold," I hoped.

Mary began using Andrew to control me when he was very tiny. One evening she became angry at me and grabbed him up, wrapped in a receiving blanket and ran outside with him and lay him down behind the back wheel of the car, threatening to run over him.

"You bring that baby in here immediately or I will call the police, and you can take your butt to jail. You know you're eighteen now; they won't take you to juvenile hall, you will go to the big jail." She brought him back. I knew she was using the baby to get at me, but I could not figure a way out of it. I would do anything for him and she knew it.

Every morning I put Andrew in the stroller and the leash on Keesha, our German Shepherd, and off we would go for our walk. They both loved it. I always said "hi" to other walkers. When Andrew was eight months old, he put up his hand and waved at a walker, and said, "hi!" From then on he said "hi" and waved at everyone we met. He was a joy. He was also my sorrow. I felt he deserved more. I knew Mary loved him but she could not seem to nurture him. It seemed that something was missing in her that was needed to mother a child.

Kim had her baby boy Michael two months and eleven days after Andrew was born. Mary and Kim had also been born two months and eleven days apart. Kim also had a cesarean. Michael and Andrew became buddies from the beginning. Kim now had two babies to care for and about. She was a good little mother and homemaker. She took her jobs seriously. When Michael was four months old, Kim and Eric got married. First they lived with Eric's parents, and then they moved into a townhouse several blocks away from us, that was owned by Eric's parents.

Without Kim, Mary now had the responsibility of taking care of Andrew during the day. When I would arrive home, she would take off, as if her work was over. Many times there was just Andrew and me. Those were precious and peaceful times.

Mary still talked about suicide, but now she would say, "If I decide to end my life, I will not leave Andrew with you, I will take him with me."

I would get very nasty with her when she said this. I knew she was capable of carrying out threats, and I became a prisoner of that thought. Would she decide to wreck the car with Andrew in it? My prison bars were my love and devotion to her son. It gave her power to hold me captive.

Shortly after Andrew's birth, I received another promotion. In addition to my duties at Friendship Village, I was to oversee a community in Yukon, Oklahoma.

I would travel there once a month for a Board Meeting and I would supervise the Executive Director there. I also received a nice raise.

In 1987 when Andrew was barely a year old, I was having pain in my upper left side. An intravenous pyelogram and other radiologic studies revealed a mass on my left kidney. The doctor thought it was a cyst, but the mass was multilocular, meaning it had many parts. The doctor said it could be a cyst, but it could also be cancer. My thoughts turned to Andrew. What would happen to Andrew if something happened to me? I had to be okay. All my kids and my brothers and sister came for the surgery. It was a scary time for all of us.

The news was good. Our prayers were answered again. It was a cyst and they were able to pluck it off. I still had my kidney and life was good. When I was faced with a chance of dying, I realized that even with all the troubles, my life had been good. I had a great job working with people I really liked. I had a loving family, and I knew Mary loved me deep down somewhere in her being. She was unable to express it.

Shortly after going back to work from the surgery, I received a call from a man I will call Victor. He was all excited. He was part owner and the managing partner of a new retirement community in Tucson. He lived near San Francisco. The Tucson community was a project that had been opened for six months but was struggling with only a few residents living there. He said he had heard about me from a man in New York and another one in Indianapolis, and he wanted me for this project. I went for an interview.

I sold my soul to the devil. He offered to double my salary plus lots of other benefits. He would pay my rent of a condo in Tucson. I really needed the money and I accepted the job. The plan was that Mary would take over the mothering of Andrew. The kids felt if Mary had to do it, she would do it. She and Andrew would stay in the house until I sold it.

I left Friendship Village in the spring of 1988. It was one of the saddest partings of my life. One of my favorite residents came up to me after I announced my leaving at a resident meeting, "You can't leave us, Gayle, you are our mother." She was crying. I cried.

The residents and staff at the Village gave me a royal send-off. There were parties and programs. The residents did a taped program, called "Gayle's Friendship Village." It was a tribute to me and a history of my eight years at the Village. The residents and staff at Friendship Village had provided me with confidence which would follow me all of my life. I felt valued by them, and I knew I would miss every one of them. I also knew that it was time to move upward and onward. There was something inside of me that caused me to want a new mountain to climb. Don't ask me why, because I don't know. Some people find satisfaction in staying in the same job forever. I wanted to stay there until I met all the goals that had been set, and then I was ready for a new mountain, especially if it doubled my salary.

It was not clear in my mind how this transition was going to take place with Mary and Andrew. I explained to Mary that I was moving to Tucson, and that she would have to step up to the plate and raise Andrew. I would put the house up for sale, and she and Andrew could stay there until it sold. I would leave enough furnishings for them and would buy new stuff for my condo in Tucson.

I had visions of a normal life in Tucson. I found a beautiful condo so close to the Catalina Mountains that it looked as if you could reach out and touch them. I had family nearby, which I thoroughly enjoyed. I enjoyed my morning walks. The Indians claimed there was something healing about the Catalinas and I felt it.

I learned right away that my boss Victor had some troublesome behaviors, but I felt I could handle anything. He could be volatile. He stayed at the community about 80 per cent of the time. One day he came in and said, "I fired one of the housekeepers."

"Who and why?" I asked.

"I caught her out in Building Ten; she was not following instructions for cleaning."

"Victor, please do not do that. You are going to get us in trouble. That is why you hired me. I can handle those things."

That is only one example of the daily interferences he provided. Sometimes I wondered why he hired me. Maybe to manage him?

13

It's Not Over Yet

Soon after I began my job in Tucson, the calls came from Mary. They were night calls for the most part. "Mom, listen to him. Andrew is crying. I don't know what to do with him."

"Why is he crying?" I would ask.

"I don't know," she answered. She was crying too. I was troubled by the thought that maybe she had hurt him, but somehow I did not think she would do that, but I would bet that she yelled at him.

"I don't know, Mom. Can we drive down there?" So here they would come, sometimes in the middle of the night. They would stay for a couple of days and then they would go back. I worried constantly about Andrew. I was beginning to understand that this hoped-for arrangement was not going to work.

Finally, on one of the night calls, she begged me, "Mom," she cried, "I can't handle this anymore, could you please take him?"

"I will take him, but first I have to arrange for a baby sitter." I knew it would be easier for me to have him with me than to suffer through these night calls and the constant worry about what was happening to Andrew. I was then 50 years old and about to become the fulltime parent of my two-year-old grandson.

One of the gals I worked with had a great sitter named Becky. Becky had a little boy named Mark who was just a little older than Andrew. She agreed to take Andrew as well. It took a little over thirty minutes to get to Becky's from my condo, but she was well worth the drive. We settled into a routine. If I had to work into the wee hours when Victor had a meeting, Andrew would stay all night at Becky's. I never worried about Andrew there and he always seemed to like going there. I could tell he adored Becky. I felt good about the child care situation, which made it possible to concentrate on work.

Sometimes I would be so tired when I arrived home, it was all I could do to get him bathed and into bed. One night it was about 9:00 when we came up the hill to home, and I remembered that I needed to buy milk. We went into the market where they had a mountainous display of Oreo cookies. "Look, Grandma, Oreo cookies!" and he tried to pick up one of the packages. The whole mountain of Oreos came tumbling down.

Andrew was terrified and began crying. Tears of exhaustion ran down my face. The nice grocery man said, "Don't cry, ma'am. I can fix it. No problem. It's okay." Sometimes a little kindness can make one fall apart. I was almost there.

I liked my job but found working with Victor impossible at times. I have often said that it is good once in awhile to work for a bad boss. It is then that you learn what *not* to do as a manager. Victor was an expert teacher at what a manager should not do. Victor often held our key staff meetings via telephone. On one such occasion we were all on the phone ready to begin; they in San Francisco and I in Tucson. We were missing their Human Resource Director, Sally, who was tied up on a phone call in an adjoining the room where Victor and his staff were.

Victor kept yelling at her to come to the phone. He began calling her names. He became loud and abusive, calling her every ugly, dirty name he could think of. I was incensed and had all I could do to be professional and courteous during our meeting.

When it was over and everyone had hung up, I called him back. "Victor," I said in my most assertive voice, "If you ever talk to me like that, I will be out of here so fast you will see my dust."

"What did I do wrong?" he asked in an innocent way.

"You treated someone very badly. I would not even treat a dog that way. I most certainly would never treat you that way. I want you to know that."

"Thank you for being honest," he said.

"You will always get honesty from me. It's the only way I know how to be." I ended our conversation. I was always hopeful that Victor would change, but I doubt he ever did. To top it off, his father was a very famous author and authority on management. I had read some of his books. Victor obviously had not.

I finally had to tell Victor, "If you want me to do this job, you must stay in San Francisco. You can come once a month to have a meeting." Surprisingly, he listened to me. We filled the place to 85 per cent in one year with a great team of people whom I had hand-picked. I knew Victor was pleased with our results, although he never once told me.

It was during that time that Mary was attending a support group to improve her parenting skills. The facilitator, Abby, was a psychologist whom Mary seemed to like. Mary related to me that she had raised the subject of her rage in her group. "I wonder where all my rage is coming from," she said. The counselor offered to meet with Mary privately to explore that issue. I paid extra for Mary to have one-on-one counseling with Abby, in the hope it would help.

I said to Mary: "You know, Mary, you have had so much counseling that you could probably teach a class or do counseling yourself."

"Abby said that I have the earmarks of an abused child and she wants to explore that with me," Mary explained. I was puzzled by that notion and doubted any abuse, but gave my okay.

After several months of Mary's counseling with Abby, I received a letter in Tucson. The letter was written to me by Abby who said, "Mary has some things she wants to ask you and tell you, but she is afraid to. So she has told them to me and I am writing them as she dictates." The letter went on to explain that Mary wanted me to know that she had been sexually abused by her dad (Raul) and she had some questions for me. There were nine questions. I felt sick to my stomach. I cannot remember all the questions. Maybe I have blocked them out. These are the ones I remember: "1. Why didn't you rescue me? 2. Did you adopt me so he could abuse me? 3. Was I a sexual substitute for you? 4. Was I the reason you slept on the couch? 5. You were the one person who could save me and you didn't … how can I forgive you?" When I received the letter I was sitting on the steps that lead from the kitchen to the living room. I flopped down on the floor and buried my head in my hands. Shock does not seem adequate for what I was feeling. I didn't cry. I think I moaned. I lay there for a half hour or so, wanting the world to go away. Wondering how this could be true. Reality was still too much for me.

Then I read the letter again. I don't remember ever having so many emotions at one time. Part of me said, "There is no way this could have happened, especially with my husband whom I trusted with our children." I took it up with Mary. She informed me, "You must have known. All mothers say they did not know abuse was going on, when they really did." I was surprised and shocked that Mary could even think that I knew what was going on. I was angry at myself for not picking up on it. I was furious at Raul.

I sat on the floor with the letter in my hand, wondering if it could be true. I thought back over the spoiling, the money he gave her, the times when Raul would baby sit with her, and I would take the other kids someplace. It never once entered my mind that Raul would molest her. I remembered one time he was called to the E.R. for a child who had been abused. He was outraged. We talked about how anyone could do such a thing.

On the other hand, I always felt that Raul had a dark cloud hanging over his head. Could this have been why? I knew he had a problem with desiring other women, but I never doubted our kids' safety with him. I knew how much he loved them.

I went on trying to remember cues that somehow I might have missed. Finally, I reasoned that if it did happen, it was good to know the source of her rage, so she could be helped. I could not get over my anger at Raul. I wanted to yell at him or have him arrested. *Could this be true, could you do this to your own daughter? Did you see what hell Mary and I have been through, and you kept your mouth shut? How could you look at yourself in the mirror every day? No wonder you had a heart attack and died. That was no doubt a heavy burden to carry. So heavy it killed you?*

When I tried to assure Mary that I had not known or ever had a thought that she was being abused, she said, "most mothers say that, when they knew about it all along."

"Well I did not. I had no idea. Why on earth didn't you come to me and tell me?" I asked.

"I could not tell you because I didn't want to betray my dad. He was my only ally in the family," she said.

It has been a mystery to me how Mary, to this day, could place her dad on a pedestal and not allow anyone to say anything against him. At the same time she vented all her rage and hatred upon me who had never done anything to her, except try and get her to mind. Now I began to see that she was taking all her rage out on me because she was mad at me for not rescuing her. She was probably thinking, "If Mom had rescued me, I wouldn't have all these problems."

I could not stomach the idea that she thought I knew about this abuse and chose to do nothing about it. Then I remembered when we gave all the kids a choice about whether they wanted to stay in Cuba City or move to Arizona, Mary was the first one to quickly say she was moving to Arizona with us. *Was this why? Did she see an opportunity to get away?*

After the initial conversation about the abuse, Mary would not discuss it with me … or anything else to do with the abuse. If I tried to bring it up, she would yell, "I don't want to talk about it!" She continued her therapy regarding the abuse. I spent many nights reviewing her growing up and Raul's parenting, trying to recall what I had somehow missed. *Was I so busy tending the forest that I missed the trees?*

I began to read anything I could find on sexual abuse. I was shocked to find out it was so common. I was watching a news report on it one night, and the newswoman said, "Can you imagine that one in four families have a child who is being sexually abused. Just open the door and look up and down the street. Now realize that one out of four of those houses are experiencing some form of sexual abuse." It made me sick.

I felt guilty that I had not been able to pick up on what was going on in my own household. I used to think that trust was a good thing. Now I realized that trust could also be foolish. I trusted Raul and look what happened.

I came to understand why Mary was so angry at me. It was because I did not rescue her. I don't think I ever convinced Mary that I had no idea she was being abused. The knowledge of the abuse caused me to be overcome with a feeling that I owed Mary big time. I owed her therapy. I owed her love and acceptance. It occurred to me that there was no "we," with Raul gone … I was it. I was all she had left. I had to help her heal her from this terrible hurt. I was her mother and I had missed it completely.

Sexual abuse victims blame themselves, I learned. They tend to think the fault is entirely theirs. They think they are bad people. They lose their self-esteem. They feel dirty. They have no respect for their own sexuality and often become promiscuous. They have a fouled-up sexual identity. They cannot seem to blame the perpetrator, only themselves. Part of the healing process is to put the blame where it belongs and direct the anger at that the perpetrator, thus eliminating the rage within themselves, or that which is directed at others. I suggested Mary write letters to her deceased father, letting him know what he had done to her life.

She could not seem to conjure up any bad feelings about her dad … only to me.

I wanted to take her in my arms and cry with her. I tried, but she would not let me.

She still refused to discuss it with me. I finally gave up trying.

I felt disgusted at Camelback Hospital. In nine months of intensive therapy, they could not discover this? I was mad at myself. I was a nurse and I knew a lot about kids … why couldn't I have picked that up? I finally wrote a letter to Raul myself to try to get rid of some of my anger:

Dear Raul,

How could you do this? All the time we were struggling for an answer to Mary's problems, you knew what the problem was and you did not come forth? Was this the dark cloud that was was hanging over you? Mary blames herself and she blames me for not rescuing her. After abusing her you gave her to me to handle the problems. Your other kids have suffered from these problems too, and you just sat there with your new life.

You must have died from carrying this deep, dark secret. You must have lived in mortal fear that one day Mary would tell all and you would be exposed. It will be a long time before I can forgive you. I will pray for God to have mercy on your soul. If you are able, you need to pray for all of us in this valley of tears.

I signed it and then destroyed it. I felt a little better after getting it off my chest.

When I told Mary's brothers about the abuse, most of them said they did not believe it (I doubt if they do to this day). That was okay. What could be accomplished by having them be angry at their dead father?

This was the most puzzling piece of the purported abuse: When I brought the subject of abuse up to Mary years later, she said the abuse never happened. First, I was shocked to hear her say that. Then I was irate … "What do you mean it never happened? What about the letter you had the psychologist write to me? What about all the hell I went through after discovering this?"

"You and the psychologist talked me into thinking I had been abused," she said without looking at me.

"Mary, what is the real reason you are now saying it never happened? You know I never talked you into it. I would have given the world not to have to believe that my own husband, whom I trusted, did this to you."

"That's all I can say. You guys talked me into it," she said.

I spoke to a psychologist about Mary's denial. She said it could have been that in Mary's mind, the truth was just too painful to bear, so she reverted to denial. I suppose there are therapists who could lead a person into thinking they had been abused. I had heard of cases where children were lead into thinking they had been abused, but Mary was not a child, she was twenty-one years old. While I wanted to believe the abuse did not happen, I found it highly unlikely that the letter to me with those nine questions was fabricated.

After a time I had come to believe that Mary *had* been sexually abused by her father for the following reason: Mary still had a lot of unresolved rage.

Why was she now denying it? 1. Perhaps it was because she felt it would spoil her name within the family. 2. Maybe she felt it would have put her in disfavor with her brothers who did not believe it. 3. Maybe she loved her dad and did not want people to disrespect him. 4. Maybe it was just easier to say that it did not happen, and then she would not have to deal with talking about it.

In looking backward, the abuse explained some things to me: Why Raul spoiled her. Why he gave her money and other gifts. Why he protected her. Why she was angry at me. Why she was filled with rage. Why she was groping for sexual identity. It explained her low self-esteem. I guess I believed that it happened, as distasteful as that thought was, because it answered a piece of the puzzle of Mary that seemed to be missing. It didn't make any sense to me that Mary dictated such a letter and then later said she was talked into it. My hope was that someday Mary would come to grips with it, so she could begin the healing process.

Meanwhile, in the other part of my life, my job in Tucson with a bipolar boss was a challenge. Victor was still the worst boss I ever had. The good thing I would say about him was that he had his PhD in marketing research, and I learned a lot about marketing, which would help in my future jobs. One day he told me about an employee whom he wanted to eliminate, "You know, I never fire anyone, I just make them so miserable they leave." I did not know how much longer I could tolerate his style. It was against everything I had been taught morally and professionally. It was clear to me now that money was not everything! I vowed that I would never take another job for the money.

14

We Move Again

Mary visited us in Tucson on a regular basis. Andrew was always glad to see her and she was happy to see him. She was proud of his intelligence and his social skills. I wanted them to be close.

A new upscale retirement community was being built by The Forum Group about five miles down the hill in Tucson. Victor was concerned about the competition. He did not know that I had received two calls from that company wanting to know if I would be interested in working for them. I had turned them down so far.

Victor suggested when the new community had their Grand Opening that we rent a hazardous waste truck and park it in their parking lot and make it look as if the community were built upon a hazardous waste dump." I laughed out loud, thinking it was a joke.

"Why are you laughing?" he said, "I am dead serious."

"You are out of your mind! I would have nothing to do with anything like that." I replied.

"Well, if you won't do that, let's go down there and take down all the license plate numbers of the people there for the open house, and then look them up their addresses … they will become *our* leads." Victor offered.

"Victor, it is not ethical. You never get ahead by doing things like that," I said. Ethics seemed to be a foreign language that he could not grasp. The good thing about Victor was that when I explained ethical things to him, he seemed to take my word for it, almost as if it had never been explained to him before.

Andrew and I had many good times together. He was a delightful child and smart. We would sing songs and recite nursery rhymes on the way to and from the baby sitter. His favorite song was "I Love You a Bushel and a Peck." Sometimes I would sing one word and he would sing the next. He could carry a perfect tune. He also had a great sense of direction. He would direct me to Becky's house, telling me each turn to make. I thought that was pretty good for a three year old. I frequently took Andrew to the retirement community and he made friends with many of the residents.

Mary called frequently to talk to Andrew. She seemed to be doing fine when we talked. I was so busy with my job and Andrew's child care that I did not think about her too much. I finally sold my home in Mesa and Mary moved into an apartment. She was a hard worker but would not consider a job such as fast food, which seemed to be beneath her. There were not a lot of high paying jobs for young people without a high school diploma. I was making into six figures and was able to help her, which was probably another co-dependent thing to do.

While in Tucson the Forum Group called me for the third time. They wanted me to interview with them for a possible position ... I figured it was for their new project in Tucson. I agreed to meet with them to see what they were all about. I really liked the key people.

They wanted me to function as a regional director over the new project in Tucson, another being built in Peoria, AZ, and another which was an acquisition in Scottsdale. After opening the Forum in Tucson, they wanted me to live in Phoenix and office out of their community in Scottsdale. I had my fill of Victor, and figured that he would begin to let me go since we were almost full. I did not want to become one of his employee victims whom he made so miserable they quit! Working with Victor and knowing he was bipolar made me wonder if Mary could possibly be bipolar. One thing for sure, they both had mood swings. In the old days of my psych nursing, bipolar was called manic-depressive disorder, which I thought was a more descriptive name, but not nearly as socially accept-able, especially if you were the one with the disorder. My previous experience with bipolar was during my three month psych training as part of my nursing program. I can remember, when in the manic phase of the disorder, a patient picked up his bed and threw it. The strength that they seemed to have in that phase was unbelievable.

I made the decision to leave Victor and the community and go with the Forum Group. My job was to open the Tucson community, and then I would move to Phoenix and open Desert Harbor. It was such a relief to have great bosses. They were professional, knowledgeable and fun. I took a thirty thousand a year cut in pay, but it was worth it. It was also good for my career to become a regional director. I had also learned a valuable lesson: There was not enough money in the world to pay me for working for and with people whom I could not trust and respect. Hopefully, I would never again sell my soul to the devil.

My social life consisted of taking Andrew out to dinner and having social times with my brothers and sisters. Occasionally, my old friend Kathy would have dinner with Andrew and me. I jokingly told my friends, "It is just as easy to fall for a rich man as a poor man." My friends were always trying to hook me up with someone. I was so afraid of making the same mistake twice, that I built a pretty good moat around me to keep safe. I did date a multi-millionaire once. I discovered that he was an ego-maniac. He talked incessantly about himself, his money, his vacations, and his airplane. I was bored stiff. Before the evening was over, he casually mentioned, "I am married, but my wife lives in Minnesota. We are estranged." Like that made it okay? That was our first and last date.

Another friend Pat matched me up with a very nice guy. We had a date and visited amicably until three a.m., during which time he told me he was gay. Nothing wrong with being gay, but he would not make a good boyfriend. I became disillusioned with the male meat market. In truth I did not have time or space for a man in my life.

I worked hard at my job and at home and I had two constant concerns … the problems associated with my daughter Mary and with raising Andrew. While my life in Tucson was good in many areas, I did not quit worrying about Mary. I suppose that Mary was suffering during that time, but at the time I never thought of *her* as suffering. I could only see how she made *our* life complicated. Since this was the first time Mary was not living with us, I began to gain some perspective about our relationship. It was still clear to me that I loved her and wanted her to be successful. I felt if she could find the right job it would help her to feel good about herself. I was always glad to see her when she came to visit and I was always glad when she left. She was high maintenance.

Mary found a job at a discount home furnishings company, where one would order furnishings from a catalog and they would be delivered to you. She seemed to thrive on that job. Since they only kept samples in inventory, the prices were good. She was strong and could lift those rolls of carpet and put them on a truck. I was thrilled for her.

I began my search for a home in the Phoenix area and found a home at the Pointe South Mountain. It was a lovely community that combined a resort, industry, apartments and single family homes on one campus. There were three swimming pools and wonderful places to walk and hike. Andrew and I moved in just before Christmas. I bought my carpet from Mary at her place of employment. I liked the new job and we settled into a routine. Andrew was in half-day kindergarten and then a bus took him from kindergarten to a nursery school where I picked him up after work.

Mary shared an apartment with a roommate, but when they had a falling out Mary would move in with us for awhile. Once she came by with a friend and said they needed a place to stay. Her new friend Suzy had given Mary some sob story. Mary told me that Suzy was down on her luck and needed a place to stay for a few days. She said she had loaned Suzy money and had even driven her to visit her mother in Colorado. Soon the police came knocking on my door looking for Suzy. I asked the policemen, "Is this a person that should not be staying in my house?"

"Not unless you want to be wiped out by her taking everything you have," the officer said. Suzy was not home at the time, but when she returned I was to call the police. Suzy must have heard that the police were looking for her because I never saw her again. Mary seemed to be a magnet for sob-story people. She would become more than a Good Samaritan for them. She became embroiled in their problems. I tried to get her to see that helping others was an admirable quality, but not if they pulled her down along with them.

Mary enrolled in a year-long school to become an interior decorator and seemed quite interested in it. I could envision her being a decorator, as she had good color sense and was a great help at decorating our different houses. She did not finish the program, however. I felt that Mary was under the influence of recreational drugs at that time, although I had no first hand knowledge of it. When it came to street drugs my knowledge was nil. I was pretty sure that none of my other kids had been involved with them. My knowledge consisted of what I had seen in movies and on TV.

The relationship between Mary and Andrew was stormy. He was a good-looking little boy and had great patience with his mother. I explained her behavior to him by telling him that she had a problem that kept her from being nice, and we should pray for her so she would get better. She was always a topic of his night-time prayers. I found a wonderful nanny named Marta who took excellent care of Andrew. She stayed with us Sunday night to Friday night, and then I would take her home. Our nanny also did all the laundry, kept the house clean, taught Andrew Spanish, and cooked! That left our weekends free to go on hikes, swim, be with family and take it easy.

The nanny told me she was afraid of Mary. Mary was scary during this time with her yelling and foul language. One day Andrew came running in from the backyard where he had been with Mary. "Come on, Grandma, into the bedroom." It sounded urgent. He grabbed my hand and pulled me. "We have to pray." He got down on his knees by the bed. I knelt down. "Dear God," he prayed, "You need to wash my mother's mouth out with soap. She said very dirty words. Amen." I was moved by his earnest prayer and I was sure God was too.

"I think God will like this prayer," I told him. About a year later, he repeated that prayer. This time his prayer was, "God, you did not get her mouth clean last time. Please, do it again!" He pleaded.

After we were settled, I got the idea of buying a decorating business and investigated owning a franchise operation. It seemed like a good idea. I thought Mary, Kim, and I could all get involved with it ... a family business. With her talent for decorating I thought Mary, who greatly needed some success in her life, could find her niche in decorating. I too liked decorating and felt it would be a business I could develop. I studied the idea for several months.

I quit my regular job and became a consultant in the same field to give me more time to study the idea of buying a franchise. The Forum Group, with whom I had been employed, became my client.

After a year of our wonderful nanny, Mary moved in with us, after having a fight with her roommate. She did not like our nanny Marta, and Marta was afraid of her. One Sunday evening when I went to pick Marta up, she said she could not come back to work because she was afraid of Mary. The order in our life came to a screeching halt. I told Mary, "Because of you, I have lost our nanny. Now you are in charge of Andrew and the house cleaning." Right.

In her desperation to maintain control or to get her way, Mary frequently used Andrew to get at me. I was getting sick of it and did not know how to stop it. Sometimes I just wanted to beat some sense into her. We frequently had yelling matches.

When she began treating Andrew badly because she was trying to get something she wanted from me, I gave in. I would do anything to keep him from being hurt. One morning she turned on Andrew and was kicking him. I had never seen her do anything like that. I ran to the phone to call 9ll and she ripped the phone out of the wall. I screamed at her, "You cannot keep me from calling the police. I will report child abuse and they will haul your butt to jail!"

Andrew was crying and hanging onto me, and she was saying to him, "Go to grandma like a big baby."

I suddenly saw an out. "I'll make a deal with you, Mary. You give me custody of Andrew and I will not report this to the police. Otherwise, I promise you that by tonight you will be in jail."

I guess Mary knew she had gone too far this time, because she said "Okay."

One thing about Mary: After she had done something terrible, she seemed get it out of her system for awhile and would be decent and likable. She was probably feeling very sorry about her behavior although she did not say that.

As soon as Mary left the house that particular day, I went downtown Phoenix to the Maricopa County Court House. I did not know how to do what I had to do, but I was determined that not another day would go by without my being Andrew's legal guardian. I looked at the Directory. I found a listing for Juvenile Court. I took the elevator up and went into an office where a young man was sitting. He was either a clerk or a secretary, and I suspected he might have been a law student. I seemed to startle him. I blurted out, "I need an emergency guardianship, and I need it today." The tears were falling down my face, and in trying to stop them I was hiccupping … an ugly sight, I'm sure. I hated the fact that I cried at the most inopportune times.

"Okay, here is what you need to do. Go down to the law library on the second floor. You need to get a form called, 'Order Appointing Guardian of a Minor,' complete it and make four copies. Bring them back up here to me, and I will get you in to see a judge. Just for the record, I am not supposed to do this." I thanked him profusely and followed his directions.

I brought the completed forms with four copies back to him. He took me right in to see a white-haired judge in a black robe who had a very kind-looking face. I felt his compassion and I wanted to cry. He asked me, "Why is it you need this order?"

"I need to be in charge of my grandson. He lives with me, and his mother comes in and out of our lives. When she wants something from me, she uses him to get it. This morning she got physical with him. If I had custody I could order her out and away from him when necessary. I'm afraid if this keeps up she will hurt him," I skimmed over the details.

"You understand that this is a temporary order. If the parents would willingly sign him over to you, it would be a lot easier to get the permanent order which would last until he is eighteen."

"I don't think I will have any trouble getting the signatures after this morning." I told him. As I was leaving, I heard him say, "Thank God for grandmothers."

I had never known who Andrew's father was. Mary verified through genetic testing that Andrew's father was Dan. Dan had been a friend and classmate of Mary's since seventh grade. Mary had told me that Dan was gay, so I was quite surprised when she identified him as the father. I liked Dan. He had been around our house frequently since junior high. Dan was good-looking and was studying to become an R.N. I was pleased to know that Andrew's dad was not some druggie bad guy. I also liked Dan's mom and she was very good to Andrew and he spent occasional weekends at her house with his other cousins.

As soon as Dan was legally identified as Andrew's father, he voluntarily began paying three hundred dollar a month to me in child support for Andrew, which helped a lot. He also began spending time with Andrew, taking him out to dinner or to a movie. Once in awhile Andrew spent a weekend with Dan.

Both Dan and Mary signed the petition for me to have permanent guardianship, and Andrew became my legal charge. I pointed out to Mary that I was legally responsible for Andrew and I would protect him from abuse, and if need be, I could and would take legal action against her. To my knowledge she never became physical with him again. However, she was quick to say awful words to him when she was angry. Her mouth was a loose cannon, firing volleys of horrible words at her targets. I knew that Mary drank alcohol and I suspected that she was born an alcoholic, but I did not know for sure that she was taking drugs. I only learned about her drug habits (for certain) much later. Call me stupid, but again, I had no experience with drugs in the family and I guess I never thought I would. I knew about the dangers of drugs, and at work we talked about how sad it was that people took drugs, but I simply did not connect drugs with Mary's behavior. After all, her behavior was not different; it was just more violent and unpredictable.

I began feeling more strongly that Mary's problem was more than being a spoiled, headstrong daughter. Why did it take me so long? The term bipolar kept coming to my mind. I talked to Mary about it. She seemed to discard the idea as one more stupid idea from me. I wanted her to be evaluated for it. She refused. Dr. Stanton had said that Mary was suffering from a Development Adjustment Reaction, in which she was kind of "stuck in the mud" and could not grow up; at least that is what I got out of his explanation. To me it sounded like a catch-all diagnosis ... one they used when they did not know what else to call it.

Mary was a hard worker when the work was her choice. You did not say, "Mary, I need your help to clean the house." You would not get it. On the other hand, she might get a notion while you were gone, to cut the grass, trim all the shrubs, and try to cook something. She did not seem to have a knack for cooking in those days. Sometimes we could not chew the food she cooked. She would be defensive and say, "Who do you think I am? Betty Fuckin' Crocker?"or "Suzie Fuckin' Homemaker?" Always the four-letter words; mostly I thought she used them for shock value or to make me mad.

Mary's language was atrocious. I pleaded with her to clean up her language for Andrew's sake. She would say, "He knows better," and he did.

He would ask, "Why does my mother say those bad words?"

"Because she never learned to talk right," I would answer, "Aren't you glad that you have been taught how to talk right?"

"Yes!" he would say. The more I begged her to clean up her language, the worse it got. I had to pick my battles with Mary, and the language problem was the least of our problems. For the most part, I just let the language go. It even rubbed off on me.

I understood the hopelessness of the physically abused housewife who kept going back for more. I realized that I was as much a co-dependent to Mary as an abused housewife might be. I even read books on it.

My close friends and family members would say, "Why don't you kick her out and change the locks?" First of all, I had tried that. We changed locks three times on three different houses. It would work for awhile. Then she would appear with no place to stay, having fought with a roommate, and I would let her in, hoping again that she had learned her lesson. I tried hard to keep a relationship between Mary and Andrew. Part of the reason I let her into my house was that I was afraid of what she would do if I did not. And then there was Andrew. He loved her and often worried about her. Children were so forgiving.

I finally made the decision to buy the decorating franchise. I talked to Mary about working in it with me. She seemed excited. We went to several meetings, took tests to see if we could do it. I used all my savings to buy it. The franchise was to be run out of our home and all the samples were to be stored in a big van which we could take out to the customer's home or place of business. The company advised us to get at least four credit cards to get us through until we started making money, which would be a several months. The franchise company took Mary and I to Baltimore for two weeks of training. I had good thoughts about how this trip could bring Mary and me closer together. We were going to be business partners. I felt optimistic.

I should have known right then and there that this business relationship with Mary would not work. She was mean and belittling to me in Baltimore, often right in class in front of everyone. She would not have a thing to do with me after class. I did not have a single meal with her in two weeks. I felt as if she were ashamed of me. She seemed to be making friends on her own. Mary could be the most charming person in the world. She never used any of her charm on me.

Back in Phoenix, I was spending less time consulting and more time trying to develop the decorating business. We had training classes once a week for fourteen weeks. Mary seemed ecstatic with the decorating.

She attended the classes every week. She seemed to be liked by the other decorators and socialized with some of them. We marketed the business by delivering flyers, and the company itself did advertising on national TV. She bought clothes so she would look professional. She had put on a lot of weight, but wore her clothes well and always looked sharp when she went out on calls.

Not being a detailed person, she made some mistakes on jobs and we lost money on them. After three months, I could see that we were going to run out of money if I did not get a regular job and get regular money coming in. I contacted the Forum Group and they hired me as a consultant out at Desert Harbor in Peoria, Arizona, about 40 miles from our home at the Pointe. Then we had money, but I did not have the time to devote to the decorating business. Mary seemed to be doing okay, if we could just make some money on the jobs. She was a born salesperson and could get the business. Her downfall was figuring jobs correctly.

While I was consulting with the Forum Group, I was contacted by Vice-President Ray Briggs, from Hillcrest, a retirement and skilled nursing company with headquarters located in the state of Washington. Ray wanted me to interview for a regional position with them to run their thirteen Arizona facilities. At first, I said, "Thanks, but I like consulting, it gives me the freedom I need right now." He kept calling. I did like him and what he said. We actually spoke for hours on the phone before I ever met him face to face. I was still not convinced that I wanted to take the job. I told him how much money it would take to get me and it did not seem to dissuade him.

I went to Tacoma and had an in-depth interview which included psychological testing. I also met with the President who was a very impressive gentleman. I believed in the same philosophy of success that he put forth. I had never been interviewed so completely! When it was over, they offered me the job. Then I had to decide if my life would let me do this. This was going to involve lots of traveling within Arizona. I would have the direct supervision of about twenty-six key employees within thirteen facilities. Andrew was in kindergarten.

Mary was entrenched in our decorating business. When I went back to Phoenix, I had a big talk with Mary. She said, "Mom, take the job. I can manage the business. I'm doing really well and I like it."

"What about the business side of it?" I asked. "You will have to make sure the bank deposits are made and money is collected and all the drapery orders are exact. The duties are huge."

"Mom, I can do it. Give me a chance."

"I will still have to sign the checks."

"You can do those in the evening or on the weekends," she said.

I took the job. Very shortly after going on with them, they decided to move the Phoenix office to Tucson, because the highest concentration of their business was there. They wanted me to move, but I could not. I loved the new challenge but was worried about keeping the home fires burning.

I began commuting every day to Tucson. One hundred miles down, one hundred back. The days were long and arduous. At least I was able to spend evenings with Andrew. I was too pooped to look into the business at night. Mary assured me all was well. I was proud of her. She had checks ready for me to sign. She always told me not to worry about a thing.

During the midst of all this, Mary surprised me one day with an announcement that she was pregnant. I hit the roof. "Mary I don't care what you do with this pregnancy … abort it, give it up for adoption, but two things I can tell you for sure: You are unable to mother a child and I absolutely refuse to raise another child for you. I cannot and will not do it." She thought about abortion. I wondered if she had other abortions that I did not know about.

Mary had an ultrasound and made a decision to put the baby up for adoption. She shopped around newspaper ads and talked to different couples who were advertising that they wanted a baby.

Mary worked with her sister-in-law Laura on this and totally left me out of the plan, which was fine with me. She decided on Glenn and Sue who lived in Rhode Island. They would pay all Mary's expenses and would agree to send photos and keep in touch with her. They came for a week before the baby was born and we got to know them. They were a very nice couple and we all felt they would be good parents. Mary was scheduled for another cesarean on Valentines Day 1993. All of us were in attendance. Sue (and maybe Glenn) was in the operating/birthing room with Mary this time.

Mary was scheduled to leave the hospital on Tuesday evening. Andrew and I went to pick her up. She said, "Mom, I am going to take the baby home with me. I cannot part with him. The social worker said not to let anyone talk me into giving him up if I didn't want to. Laura (her sister-in-law) has gone to get a car seat for the baby."

My heart sank. "Mary, he is a lovely baby and I love him too, but you are in no shape to care or support or raise this baby. He deserves to have a mom and dad who will love him and give him a normal home. Glenn and Sue seem perfect."

"I told Glenn and Sue that I needed just one night with him. They will call me in the morning." Mary persisted.

Since we had to wait and since we had not yet eaten, Andrew and I went to a Chinese restaurant nearby that we frequented. The waitress recognized us and greeted Andrew. "Andrew, how are you? You are getting so big! How old are you now?"

"I am five," he smiled.

"Do you have any sisters or brothers?" she asked.

"I have a brother, but we are giving him away," he replied. I looked away and the waitress did not push for details. Andrew and I discussed why Adam was going to live with other parents. I explained that we were not giving him away—we were giving him a life. He seemed to understand. I wanted to make sure that he knew we were not going to "give *him* away".

We took Adam (Glenn and Sue had named him) home … a trip filled with trepidation on my part. What would I do if Mary absolutely refused to let him go? I told Mary that she was going to take care of Adam that night and from then on, for ever how long she kept him. I put Adam near her bed so she could hear him. Of course, I did not sleep. I prayed, "God, please let Adam be with Glenn and Sue." I could see that they already loved him.

In no time at all Adam began to cry. At first she must have picked him up because he only cried for a short time. In about half an hour he started in again, this time for real. I looked at my watch. He needed to have a bottle. How long could I let this newborn cry? Pretty soon she cried out, "Mom, I just can't do it. Please come and get him. I will let Sue and Glenn take him home with them tomorrow."

I went in and picked up this sweet, newborn baby, my grandchild. I held him and fed him and cuddled him and loved him and told him, "You are going with Glenn and Sue tomorrow because we love you and we know they will be good parents. We will always love you too. You will stay in our hearts."

Mary kept her word. Glenn and Sue became Adam's parents the next day. I felt relieved and happy for Adam. Mary grieved and had lots of guilt and sorrow over giving Adam up for adoption. Glenn and Sue were good about keeping in touch. They moved to Wisconsin, near Milwaukee. When I went to visit my son Steve in Madison, Glenn and Sue invited Andrew to spend a week with his brother Adam. When we picked Andrew up, I could plainly see that Adam had a happy home. I prayed that Adam did not inherit Mary's bad traits; only her good ones.

15

Financial Chaos

My new job was consuming. I worked long hours. It was really a communication job. I spent most of my time on the phone speaking with those I supervised. There were also meetings in Tacoma. After six months of driving back and forth from Phoenix to Tucson every day, I felt like I could not do it anymore. Mary was going to have to take over the responsibility for Andrew, except on weekends. I began driving to Tucson on Monday morning and driving back to Phoenix Friday evening. Andrew was not thrilled with the situation and said, "Grandma, I liked it better when you were here every day." I was signing lots of checks for decorating payments, but I was making good money and was building up my savings.

I should have been suspicious when on the weekends I wanted to review all the decorating stuff. Mary would say, "Mom, you've had a hard week, just relax, I have everything under control." I was grateful … and was being my usual trusting, tired self. We discussed her current clients in a general sense, but not in detail. When I would ask questions about specific accounts, she felt I was criticizing, so I would back off.

After months of working for Hillcrest, I took a long weekend off. During that time I had literally let Mary manage our finances, including bill paying and banking. On my long week-end off I opened the mail for the first time in months. The first thing I opened was the bank statement. My balance was a minus twenty-eight dollars. *Why didn't they transfer the money from savings to cover it? I had that kind of coverage. Why was I overdrawn anyway?* I looked through the checks and found four checks which *I* had not signed. It looked like my signature, but I had not signed them. They added up to nine hundred dollars. *What was going on?* My heart was racing. *There had to be a mistake, and where did these checks come from that I did not sign?* There could only be one answer. Mary. Forgeries. I took the statement and checks and ran up to the bank. I found out that I was in bad shape.

My savings account had been depleted by Mary using my debit card, which I allowed her to use for the business.

I don't know which emotion I felt the most, anger or fear. Here I thought I was doing so well. I kicked myself for not paying better attention. I trusted people too much, even after they had used me. I had done it with Raul and I had done it with Mary over and over. Now what was I going to do? I began the investigation into previous bank statements. There was almost $5,000. in forgeries over the last few months. The signatures were so close to mine. *How did she do it?* Also, I could not find evidence that she had paid our franchise dues and charges, and I knew we would lose the decorating business if they were not paid.

I loaded the forgeries into a brief case and took them to an attorney specializing in fraud. He told me, "To be honest with you, while this may seem like a huge thing to you, it is really small fish to the County Attorney. You could prosecute, but it will end up costing you more than the $5,000 and it would take forever before it would come up in court. And it does not sound as if your daughter has any funds to pay you back? Also, there is the matter that you gave her your checkbook and agreed for her to manage your business. The judge may think you had it coming."

I felt I was in another hopeless situation. I confronted Mary. It was not a pretty conversation. I was in no frame of mind to be reasonable. Talk about rage … I had it. "How could you do this to me? I spent everything I had to get into this business, mainly because I thought you would be really good at it, and so that when I retired, I could do it too. So what have you done? You have depleted my checking and savings and have forged checks on me. I shudder to think what else you may have done that I don't know about yet. Pack your things and get out of my house and out of my life." She offered no excuses. She got her stuff and left. We changed all the locks … again.

I called the Human Resource Director of Hillcrest in Tacoma. I told her I was really needed in Phoenix because of family issues. She suggested that I work out of my home. "You have a computer, fax and copy machine. Most of your work is either in a facility or on the phone; you can base all of that from home, at least until you get things ironed out." I felt much relief and thought perhaps I could straighten out my scrambled life after all.

I spoke to my staff at the office in Tucson, and they did not see a problem with the new arrangement. I would still be visiting all my communities and would come to the Tucson office once a week.

On Monday, I was working from home. I had called all the facilities and had fielded several concerns before 10:00 A.M.. My boss Ray called me. "Where are you?" he asked.

"Working at home."

"Working on what?"

"On Hillcrest business."

"Like what?"

"Well, so far I have spoken to all those I supervise and have fielded two concerns. Ray, I am having some problems at home that are going to require me to work out of my home office for awhile. I need to be in Phoenix more, so I have my evenings to take care of business here."

"I don't want you working out of your home."

"Why not?"

"I want you in the facilities even more than you are now. You bring a kind of magic to the buildings when you go into them. We need to have more of that. I don't want you in *any* office very much."

"Ray, you don't understand the nature of my job. I am on the phone constantly. It is not unusual for me to have fifty phone calls a day. Many of them are from you! I can't go into a facility and be on the phone the whole time I am there. That just keeps the Executive Director from doing his job. I can be on the phone here as easily as I can in Tucson."

"No, I can't allow it."

I was feeling frustrated at how the conversation was going. "How about just trying it for a few months? Maybe I can get things straightened out here by then."

"No, I can't do it."

"Ray, please don't do this. If I can't work it out I may have to resign."

"Well, don't do anything today. Think about it until Tuesday and then give me a call," he said.

Now, on top of having to find out what terrible shape I was in financially, I was going to have to quit my job? Could I turn the decorating business into a successful venture? I had too much invested in it to throw it away. I went to Tucson on the following Tuesday and called Ray.

His first words were, "Have you made the decision to move to Tucson?"

"Ray, there is no way I can move to Tucson." I was disappointed that he had not budged.

"Why not?"

"I have a grandson in Phoenix, I haven't even owned my house for a year, and I am having big problems with my daughter." I did not go into detail. I was ashamed of what had happened and did not think I needed to explain all my dirty laundry to him. "I need to be in Phoenix. Please try to understand. Remember, you told me before I was hired that family has to come first and the job second." I was pleading.

"*You* need to understand that your needs are counter to what I feel our company needs are at this time," he stated.

"Then I will fax you my letter of resignation." I put the receiver down. I could not continue talking. There was no use continuing anyway, his mind was made up, and I was choked up with tears. I did not want to show him my female weakness for tears.

I completed the resignation letter with a thirty-day notice, and faxed it to him within ten minutes. I told the staff, "I am going for a walk. I won't have my phone. If Ray or anyone else calls, I am not available."

I walked and cried. Was this a power struggle, or was he right that the corporation could not allow me work at home. Maybe he did not trust that I would spend adequate time on company business. He did not know how dedicated I was to every job I had ever had. I always gave more than was required. *Oh well, it's their company, and they can do whatever they want.*

Ray telephoned while I was out walking, and when he found that I was not available, he became upset, according to the staff, and faxed an acceptance of my resignation. I had done a super job for this company. I knew I had. We had built a strong, cohesive team who was doing well and seemed to be enjoying their work. We were on our way to accomplishing much more. *Could he not see that?*

Even though I gave a thirty-day notice, I agreed to stay for sixty days, until they could find a new Regional Director. A couple weeks after my resignation, Ray called and said, "I have a petition signed by your administrators who want me to keep you on. So I will ask one more time, are you ready to move to Tucson?"

"I appreciate their efforts, Ray. I would if I could, but I can't."

"This is your last chance."

"I know." I was trying to leave on the best of terms. I had never left a job that I could not go back to. I did not believe in burning bridges. I loved that job and it added to my anger at Mary for the trouble that was causing me to have to quit. I felt anger and self-recrimination at myself for neglecting to supervise Mary's work. *How could I be so stupid?*

So I left Hillcrest on the best of terms … with going away parties and dinners. Again it was a hard parting for me. I was cemented into that job and our team members were very close. (Several years later Ray saw me at a meeting and told

me that letting me get away was one of the biggest mistakes he had ever made).
For both of us.

Andrew said, "Grandma, please don't ever go away like that again. I don't want you to work in Tucson anymore." At least from Andrew's view point I had made the right decision.

"I won't," I promised. "I am going to be working right here."

Now the real work began of finding out where I was financially. The credit card bills were up to $29,000. The total amount of forgeries was $5,000. Mary had used a franchise program which was to give credit to our customers, and had fictitiously gotten $15,000 from there. Even I could not figure out how she did that. The franchise dues had to be paid. I was in a state of panic. I needed to pull myself together so I could pull the business together. The business represented everything that I had earned and saved.

Mary had left several decorating jobs in mid-air. One job was custom-lined draperies for a residence. The installer called me. The drapes had been mis-measured and none of them could be used. I went to the customer and assured her that we would make it right. That snafu cost me $5,000 including the remake. They were beautiful custom draperies with full linings which had to be scrapped.

I borrowed money from insurance policies, took my IRA out of Hillhaven, took money from every little thing I had for retirement. At the rate I was going, I would not live long enough for retirement anyway. I paid off what debt I could, kept the utilities paid, and tried to get the business going. I found one credit card that I did not know existed. Mary had opened that card in my name, forging my signature. It was maxed out at $5,000. I spoke to them and they were the only card company that said they would go after *her*, and I would not have to pay. The other credit card companies required that I prove that my company did not receive any benefit from their use. I could not prove that. Most of the card companies were brutal.

Bit by bit, the story emerged from Mary about what had happened to cause her to deplete my finances. It seemed she met up with another woman named Vicki. Vicki was a drug user, a drug dealer, and a gambler … and her lover. The fact of finding out that Mary was gay did not bother me. That was the least of our problems. That my money was used for their fun, gambling and drugs made me livid. They lived high for awhile. She even bought a car for Vicki. I had met Vicki, who was an electrician. She too could be very charming and even did some electrical work for me. I had no idea about her vices at that time.

I had gone from having perfect credit when I bought my house to huge credit balances on every card, and now I had no immediate income, except decorating. I also had some unhappy decorating customers. Luckily my contacts in the retirement field were contracting with me to do some decorating work in their communities. I had trouble keeping my focus on the business. Isn't there a saying that it is hard to drain the swamp when you are up to your ears in alligators? That's where I was, in the swamp. Our decorating business was designed so that you received a deposit up front to cover the expenses of material. When the job was completed and the customer was satisfied, you received the final payment. When working with corporations, I would often not receive my final payment until 60-90 days after job completion.

I don't know how to explain my state of mind during this time, except to say that I was functioning on the outside, but inside I was a zombie. I was void of feeling and enthusiasm. I had lost my ability to dream. I was no longer thinking in a success mode. I was thinking that nothing was ever going to work out for me. All the ways I had pumped myself up in the past did not seem to work anymore.

One day I ran out of gas while going to a decorating job and realized that I did not have any money or any credit to buy gas. I had closed every credit card and I did not even have money for the pay phone. For the first time in my life I knew what it was to be penniless. I could not even pay for a phone call. I sat in the car crying for close to an hour. I was so mad at myself. *How could I be so stupid as to let this happen to me?* I finally went into the grocery store and said, "May I please use your regular phone? I forgot my purse and I need to call my daughter in law?" They let me use the phone to call Liz, Bruce's wife. In a breaking voice I said, "Liz, I ran out of gas and I don't have any money."

"Hang on, Mom. I'll be right there.

Liz came right away and insisted I take their gas and oil credit card and she said, "Keep this until you don't need it anymore." She also gave me $20. I vowed that somehow I would get out from under this. I was grateful for Liz and Bruce and for my close friends who supported me. Most of all I was thankful for my faith. I watched the Hour of Power every Sunday morning. Then I would watch the North Phoenix Baptist Church service. Then Andrew and I would go to the Catholic Mass and he would go to the spiritual education program for children. I listened over and over to the tape, *The Power of Positive Thinking*, by Norman Vincent Peale. I finally wore it out. One of the hardest things to get over was the self-reproach. *How could I be so naïve as to think everything was okay?* As hard as I tried, I could not get enthusiastic again … I could not get my dreams back. Many times I felt like I had fallen into a black hole and every time I tried to crawl out, I fell back down.

I sat Andrew down and explained our situation to him, "Honey, we are going to have to change the way we live. Grandma has run out of money. We won't be eating out and we will have to make do with what we have. We won't be buying new things for awhile. It will take Grandma a while to get back to where we were. Do you understand?"

"It's okay, Grandma. We can do it," he answered.

He never asked for anything after that. He didn't ask for treats at the grocery store. He didn't ask for new clothes. If I purchased something, he would say, "Are you sure we can afford that?" He was a cool kid and a comfort to me.

One day we went out for a walk in the mountain preserve. Out of the blue he asked me, "Can you be my mom?"

"You already have a mom; I am your ever-loving grandma."

He thought for a few moments and then said, "You're the mom of my heart."

I hugged him with tears in my eyes, as I wondered and worried how all that he had been through would affect his life.

Bruce and Liz became the "back-up" parents for Andrew. When I had to travel or could not pick him up from day care, they pitched in. I wanted Andrew to spend as much time with them as possible because they were a role model for a happy family. They did lots of neat things with their kids and included Andrew. Liz was a strict disciplinarian and made the kids tow the line. In later years I told her it was like "boot camp." When Andrew was slipping, I would say to her, "Liz, can Andrew come to boot camp?" Their son Alex was one and a half years younger than Andrew, and Kelsey was seven years younger than Andrew. I loved baby-sitting with Alex and Kelsey when I could.

I tried valiantly for about six months to turn my decorating business into a profitable business. If I had not been so down and out, perhaps I could have done it. Success breeds success and I was no longer operating in the success mode. I had a recurring dream that I was caught in quicksand and would wake up struggling. Maybe if the business had not been in such a mess. I could have made it work. Maybe if I had been a better decorator it would have worked. Maybe if there had not been so much pressure from creditors, I could have succeeded. I didn't know. I knew that it took money to make money. I did not have money to buy the new samples or to pay for advertising.

I had to give it up. I was unable to sell the van, so I had to let it go back … another black mark on my credit. The decorating franchise did all they could do to help, they absorbed the $15,000 fictitious credit Mary had developed through the decorating franchise. The scary thing to me was that my heart was not in taking on a new job. Where and how was I going to get my enthusiasm and positive attitude back? How do you find your dreams once you have lost them?

16

The Phoenix Bird

In Egyptian legend there was a phoenix bird that burned itself up when it became 500 years old. From its ashes another phoenix bird arose. I valiantly tried to be a phoenix bird. In 1995 I got a call from the company I used to work for at Friendship Village. They asked me if I would help them out by doing some consulting in New Jersey, thirty minutes from Philadelphia. They had taken on a management project there and said they could use my help. It was half as much money as I had made with Hillcrest, my previous job, but I accepted. I had to make some arrangements for Andrew. Liz and Bruce would help out, but Andrew needed to get to school and back and have someone there when he got home.

Mary was in communication with Andrew. She said she was through with Vicki and that Vicki was out of her life. In my fuzzy mind, (or perhaps I was just plain wacky at this point) I decided that Mary owed me big time. She would have to come back and watch the house and Andrew when he was not with Liz and Bruce. Mary and I agreed that enough problems had happened, and this was her chance to make it up to me. She seemed sorry and assured me that Vicki was out of her life completely. She bad-mouthed Vicki and poured out all the sordid details of their stormy relationship. Never did I hear her say that she herself was on drugs, even when I asked. She admitted to alcohol use and how bad it was for her and how she had quit using alcohol. When Mary wanted you to believe something, she could be more convincing than any person I have ever known. As I told you she should have been in sales.

I forgave Mary again. Partly because I loved her and wanted to believe her, partly because it was my nature to be forgiving, partly because I needed her help, and partly because I was not thinking clearly. I had been raised to turn the other cheek and forgive, forgive, forgive. That is the way my mother was. Many times my close friends would say, "How could you forgive her again?" I either had a good grasp on the meaning of forgiveness, or I was just plain stupid.

I went off to New Jersey for a three-month stint. The bustling town was a blue collar industrial city. The retirement village was within the city limits and only thirty minutes from Philadelphia. It was a nice-looking village set in the tall pines. I learned why New Jersey was called the garden state ... it was early spring and everything was beginning to bloom. I would walk around looking at trees, bushes, and flowers blooming. Many houses sported spring banners, adding a colorful touch. "Maybe this is a place for healing," I hoped. I lived in an apartment in the retirement community, just like the residents. The residents were kind to me and often took me sight-seeing on weekends. It was a peaceful existence. I worked hard during the day, and then relaxed in the evening and on weekends. I thought of my free time as a retreat for healing.

I was keeping a journal and writing some poetry. I wrote:

Spring in South Jersey

My heart feels light and happy
As I look down the street
At a dozen shades of flowering trees,
As the spring flags wave hello.
The dogwoods, cherry blossoms, and flowering pear
Are blooming above, while tulips, daffodils,
Pansies, azaleas, vie for color spots.
Spring speaks to me here in the tall pinelands.
God sent me to South Jersey
To feel the incredible spring
And to smell the flowers
And to walk in the woods.
He sent me to be with the Harvest Villagers,
To feel their hospitality and care,
Their love for and pride in their Village.
To share with them a moment in time.
God sent me to South Jersey
To remember spring in all its glory,
Because I had forgotten spring
And its message of hope after winter's pall.

On April 19, 1995, while I was working in Jersey, the Murrah building in Oklahoma City was bombed. When that terrible thing happened, the first thing I thought of was my family. When such tragedy occurred it seemed to crumble the tent of confidence under which I lived from day to day … the feeling that our world was basically okay. I called all my kids just to hear their voices.

I could not break myself away from the television coverage. I cried and grieved over those killed, especially the children. I grieved for the families of the dead and injured, I grieved for my own losses. It seemed as if this terrible event provided me with an acceptable vehicle with which to grieve my own losses. I let it all out. I wrote more poetry, which I frequently did during stormy times.

The Bell Tolls in Oklahoma

I feel your pain as I am fixed to CNN.

I am overwhelmed at this travesty;

I cry as babes bleeding and worse are rushed out;

I stare in disbelief; the authors American? UNamerican!

I listen to arguments that we need better and more security.

I learn of militia groups who are in training against government.

At night I wonder about the life path of one who could do this.

Do we as Americans contribute to the making of such a demon?

I feel in my heart that the perpetrators do not know love,

Or at least they fail to absorb love and what it means;

For to love, is to value life, to nurture it, to care for it.

Did we cause them to devalue life in some Nam jungle?

I feel such urgency to get all those who hate, back from hell.

Hatred breeds death, sorrow, pain, bleeding children.

How can we get back to the basics: love, respect, life values?

Do we need more security? No, we need to love more and better.

We need to make sure no kid grows without love,

NO teen-ager goes without a dose of it daily …

Those who don't feel love can't love anyone else.

It will take us all, loving each other, and loving those hardest to love,

Or the tragedy will continue …

When I returned to Phoenix, I found out that Mary was not through with her girlfriend Vicki. We had another big fight and I kicked her out again. At least I was feeling more settled. I had worked through the loss of my finances. The only problem was that I could not get my dreams back. At least that is what I called it. Others may have called it situational depression. I could not feel that old enthusiasm and creativity which had been such a big part of me and my career. It was as if there was a dead space in me and I could not revive it. And, of course, I was still in the hole financially, which did not help.

One day a realtor came knocking on my door at the Pointe. He said he had a client who wanted to buy my house. I had thought about selling it, but needed to paint it and do some small repairs before I put it on the market. The realtor said, "My client wants to live here at the Pointe. He is an airline pilot and this is a great location for him. He likes this particular model. He would like to buy it as is. We would like to make you an offer."

I enjoyed living there and I especially liked the house, but this would give me some cash to help pay bills. Besides, my homeowners' dues were coming up and I did not have the $1300. "O.K," I said, "Make me an offer." They made me an offer on a Friday. I made a counter-offer on Monday, and they accepted on Tuesday.

The buyer wanted a fast closing, so Andrew and I began looking for a place to rent. With my credit, I knew I could not buy at that time. We found a nice three-bedroom house at The Lakes in Tempe. Because of my credit problems, I had to have a co-signer. My son Steven, the anesthesiologist, co-signed for me. It was another dose of humility for me. I had gone from being a very successful professional woman with perfect credit, to needing to have my son co-sign for me to rent a house. Humility was painful.

We moved to The Lakes in Tempe and liked it. It was a planned community with a recreation center and pool and two big lakes. It also had a cute little coffee café called Coffee Grounds. Daughter Kim came to live with us temporarily after a divorce from her husband. She had a job and was a great help with Andrew. Our landlords were good people. Andrew was just a block from school. He was then in fifth grade.

Mary was popping in now and then to see Andrew. She sometimes ran errands for me. She could be a big help when she wanted to be. She seemed happy to see Andrew. She would wash the car and take my clothes to the cleaners. Of course, she had no money and no job.

While I was in Tucson for a meeting she totaled my Camry; although it was not her fault. She was lucky not to have been killed. Our insurance company saw that we got another car and then they went after the other insurance company. I don't know if the other company paid and Mary used the money; however, when I called them, they said it the claim had been settled. My insurance company never received their payment. Mary obviously took the payment. She always had an answer. Or she became so enraged at the questioning of her integrity that I would back off. Another theft of funds.

Was I afraid of Mary? Yes, there were times when I was afraid of her, but I worked hard not to let her know that. If Mary sensed you were afraid, it seemed to make her angrier and then she was unable to stop. It worked best if you said loudly, "I will not allow you to hurt me!" If she sensed I was afraid, she seemed to wield that power against me. In many ways I was a prisoner. Was I a prisoner because I wanted peace? Or was I a prisoner because I was afraid of being killed? Or was I a prisoner because I could not figure out what the heck to do about her behaviors? Perhaps I was a prisoner because I loved her and could not walk completely away.

When Mary was little she could always find a way around obstacles that anyone put in front of her. She had become more adept at it in adulthood. She also became more violent in adulthood. After years of living with the violence, I would do almost anything to keep peace, even if it meant giving into her. I think I had developed a loser attitude of "Nothing is going to work anyway; so it doesn't matter what you do."

I have played down my increasingly angry responses to Mary's outbursts and manipulations. I was became a screaming wild woman, nearing the end of my rope. I wanted Mary out of my life and out of Andrew's life. He was beginning to have problems at school, mostly from not paying attention. I asked the counselor to speak with him. Afterward, she called me.

"Andrew is so worried about his mother that he is finding it hard to concentrate," she told me. "Evidently Mary has shared with him that her life is so bad she doesn't want to go on living. He is worried that she will kill herself. I have told Andrew, and I hope that you will reinforce it, that "Mary is your mother and you, Andrew, are the child. It is not your duty to worry about her. She is supposed to worry about you. She is an adult and she can take care of herself."

We worked hard on this with Andrew. I told Mary not to share things like that with him. I said, "Mary, you are the mother and Andrew is the child. You cannot confide in him as if he is your mentor. It is hurting him at school and is hurting his confidence that things are okay." She was good about it after that.

I went to Tucson one weekend for a wedding and to visit family. Andrew was staying with Bruce and Liz, and Kim now had her own apartment. Mary had shown up unexpectedly again and was living with us for what she said would be a very short time. When Mary asked me what time I would get back from Tucson, I told her that I would be home around 4:00 P.M.. My plans changed and I arrived home at 1:00 P.M..

When I let myself into the house from the garage there was a flurry of activity. There was Mary's old girlfriend Vicki, the gambling druggie who helped put me into financial ruin, in my bed! I lost it. "Get the hell out of my house. How could you possibly show your face here after what you did?" I was screeching at the top of my voice. Mary was frantically trying to shut me up.

"Mom, chill out. You are acting crazy." That added to my fury. "Get out of here both of you. I am going to call the police. I went to the phone. Mary grabbed it out of the wall and broke the phone. I went to the other phone. She grabbed it and broke it too. She began hitting me. I ran outside and she ran right after me. There was a neighbor guy about twenty-something years old outside in his yard. I pleaded, "Will you please call the police for me? I need help."

He answered, "Quiet down, will you, we have guests!"

I staggered through the greenway to the sidewalk, which lead over to the "Coffee Grounds" café, where I called my son Mike. He said, "Stay right there, Mom, I will be right over."

Mary and Vicki came driving by and Mary hollered at me. "Mom, let's talk."

"No, Mary. No more talk. Get out of my life. Leave us alone. You show up and I call the cops." They finally left.

The following Saturday morning the hospice for which I was Executive Director was having a function at a resort in Phoenix. I needed to be there. It was about 7:00 A.M. I was the only one at home and I was half dressed, when I heard the front door open with a key. "Mom, it's Mary. I need to talk to you." She must have copied our house key.

"Get out of my house!" I screamed.

"Mom, we need to talk. I need some money for a place to stay."

"That's your problem. I am not giving you money. I don't care if you sleep in the street. Just get out of here!"

She came closer. "Mom, you are acting stupid. Just listen to me," she yelled.

"Listening to you has gotten me into every kind of trouble. I'm through."

This statement enraged her. She grabbed me and threw me on the bed. I fought back. I was able to get up. I ran into the bathroom and tried to close the door. She forced it open. When she was in a rage she had the strength of a giant. She gave me a big push. I fell into the shower and hit my head and my hip. I lay there in the corner of the shower dazed and whimpering. At that moment I felt my life would never be right until one of us died. I wished she had killed me so that I would be out of this agony once and for all.

"Get up!" she said. "You are not hurt." She hesitated slightly and then she left. I examined my body and decided that I did not break a hip. I had a big bump on the back of my head and I felt a little dizzy. My immediate thought was that I *had* to function on this day that was going to last into at least 11:00 P.M. I could cover up all my bruises. The challenge was going to be to act as if nothing had happened when I was with my co-workers. I called Mike to see if he could again change the locks that day. He said he would and he did.

I had not lived at The Lakes very long and I was feeling humiliated that once again a neighbor had witnessed violence coming from our house. I was also highly insulted that my neighbor had been unwilling to call the police for me. Worse was the way he looked at me, as if I were trash with whom he would not associate. That was one neighbor I did not care to know. Oh yes. Humility again. Was part of humility learning not to care what other people thought of you? I suppose it was. I wanted to yell out to them, "We are good people; we just have a crazy daughter! It could happen to you!"

After this incident I lost all the ground that I had gained emotionally. Would my life ever be right? Was this my destiny? I performed well that day in spite of my aches and pains from that morning. I still had two lives. If my professional colleagues knew in what hell I lived, they would not believe it. Most of the time I did not believe it myself.

When I arrived home that night, I examined the bruises on my body. Thank God they could all be covered with clothing. I went to the court to see about getting a restraining order. As the judge told me, "A restraining order is just a piece of paper. It may not deter someone from coming near you, especially if they want to hurt you. What it does do, is give you the right to have them arrested for disobeying the court order." Also, the order had to be delivered to her and I had no idea where she was. I thought about it and decided that a restraining order would not stop Mary. All the king's horses and all the king's men could not stop her.

My boys were older now. I was the grandmother of eleven grandchildren. I knew that Mary's sister and brothers worried I might get seriously hurt or even killed by Mary. There was something inside of me that believed Mary would never kill me. I hated her behavior, but I still loved her. No matter how many times I wanted her out of my life, I could not give up on her. I was all she had. I kept forgiving.

Again I remembered from my child psychology classes, "Separate the doer from the deed." That was a hard concept for my older kids to grasp. I made up a song about this for my grandchildren. It went like this to the tune of Davy Crockett: "I love you when you're good, and I love you when you're bad. I love you when you're happy, and I love you when you're sad. I don't always like the things that you do ... but ... I'll always ... love you! My grandchildren loved this song, especially Alex, who would ask me sing it over and over again. That was a song about unconditional love. It separated the doer from the deed. Kids grasped that thought.

I had still not paid off all the credit cards from the decorating fiasco but I was making progress. I had paid off two of them plus the state taxes that Mary didn't pay. It was hard to pay credit cards off by paying the minimum. I figured that I would have to live to be one hundred and twenty years old before I would get them paid.

17

Christmas, Guns, and SWAT Team

Mary did not live with us anymore. She lived various places with various friends, mostly with her friend Ann. Ann and her family seemed to accept Mary as she was. I didn't know how she behaved with them, but they seemed to like her. *There was a little girl, who had a little curl, right in the middle of her forehead. When she was good, she was very, very good, and when she was bad she was horrid.* That was our Mary. She was out of our lives for the time being. Our whole family began to relax a little. I didn't hear from her often. When I did, I was afraid she was going to ask for money or try to come back home. While Mary was gone, Andrew and I missed the *good* part of her, but we liked our peace. I did not want her to come home, but I never stopped praying for her. With help from the Hour of Power and my St. Timothy's Church, I was able to work through my feelings and had *almost* forgiven her. Forgetting would take longer.

I was facing a big rent increase at the Lakes, so I decided to try to buy a house. My credit was repaired enough to swing it. We found just the house for us in Chandler, Arizona, just outside Phoenix and Tempe. We moved into it in September of 1997. It was not as nice as previous homes I had owned but we liked it. It was a good house for family, and it was a good neighborhood for Andrew. It felt good to have get-togethers without fear of a blow-up. I didn't think Mary knew that we moved or where we lived … I hoped. In my entire span of parenthood, this was the first time I felt Mary and I were going our separate ways, although I knew she could find us if she wanted. She was very resourceful.

I heard that Mary had moved to Las Vegas with her friend Ann. I could only imagine what she was into there. I didn't like to think about it. Someone in the family told me they had heard she was involved in an escort business. I didn't know what that meant exactly, and I didn't want to know. My other kids and some of Mary's acquaintances would feed me bits of information from time to time about Mary having been involved in prostitution, drugs, abortions ... she had apparently done it all. Where would it end? I half expected someone to come knocking on my door to tell me that someone had killed her.

On December 23rd 1999 we had our house all decorated for Christmas, the shopping was done, and I was preparing for our annual family get-together on Christmas Eve and for a trip after Christmas. My oldest son Steve, his wife Kelly, and their two boys were taking me to Hawaii. I had never been there and I was pretty excited about it. My boys always did kind things for me. I was proud of them and the parents they had become. Steve frequently sent me money. It was always when I needed it most. He seemed to know, without being told, when I could use an extra financial boost. Andrew was a teen-ager. He would stay with Bruce and Liz while I was away.

At dawn on December 23 the door bell rang. My heart sank, thinking there must be some emergency. I peeked out the side window by the door. There was Mary with several full garbage bags and a big suitcase. Without thinking I gave a negative response: "What are you doing here?" I said in a not-happy-to-see-you voice.

"Is that any way to greet your daughter?" she asked, tears welling.

"What happened? I asked, making no effort to open the screen door.

"Ann and I had a fight. Look, Mom. It's Christmas. I haven't seen my son in a long time," she said with her lips quivering.

I took a look around my living room. There was our beautiful Christmas tree and all the presents. The house was all decorated. We were blessed. Maybe for the first time in my life I felt sorry for Mary, and saw what little she really had. What she had was probably right there in those bags. Could I say "There is no room in the inn?" I opened the door and gave her a hug. "Come on in." I loved her. To tell you the truth I always felt that part of our family was missing when Mary was gone, even while I was enjoying the peace.

The next day was Christmas Eve and the Lagman family get-together was at our house. We were up early to get things ready. My friend Megan came to help. I went all out for Christmas Eve. Our tradition was to have homemade chili, shrimp cocktail, dips, veggies, ham sandwiches, cookies, candies, and peanut butter. The boys loved peanut butter and French bread with their chili!

Mary was a big help in getting us ready for the party. Then she said, "Mom, I am not comfortable being here with the family tonight. The boys will be upset that I am here." I knew she was right and besides I was afraid of a blow up that would ruin Christmas Eve for all of us.

"What would you do?" I asked.

"If I could use your car I would go over to some friends, and then come back when everyone is gone," she offered.

"Our evening is usually over early because of all the kids, so I am planning to go to midnight mass. You would have to be back by 10:30 so I could get to church and get a seat." I cautioned.

"No problem. I'll be here."

Mary went out one door and the family began arriving through the other door. We had our usual wonderful time. I told them, "Mary rang the doorbell at 4:00 A.M. yesterday; she had a fight with Ann in Las Vegas and arrived here with all her belongings."

"Where is she now?" Bruce asked.

"Mary knew that you all would not want to see her, so she went to visit friends," I said.

"So what will happen now, Mom? Are you going to let her back into your life?" Bruce asked, sounding disappointed in me.

"I know I can't. But when I saw her standing out there, knowing it was Christmas and she was all alone, I couldn't shut the door in her face." I thought they understood, but I could see they didn't like it. I'm sure they were afraid of history repeating itself. As I was.

The family was all gone by 9:30 P.M.. At 10:30 P.M. I began calling Mary on the cell phone. She did not answer. I kept trying. I was getting upset. Same old, same old, I thought. I finally went to bed and lay there wondering if she had been in an accident. She was so convincing when she said that she would be back on time. But then Mary was always convincing. She was an expert. I had been had … one more time.

As I said my prayers, I tried to recall the scripture about how many times you were to forgive a person. Was it seventy times seven? That would be four hundred-ninety. I thought I was almost there.

I don't know what time Mary came in, but she slept all the next morning while we had our Christmas. Andrew and I went to church. When Mary woke up she was like a bear cat. I guessed that she was hung over, maybe even had some drugs. She was totally different than she had been on Christmas Eve day. I did not want to foul up Christmas by fighting with her, so we just stayed out of her way. In the early afternoon she said, "I left my wallet at my friend's house and I need to go get it. I need to borrow the car."

"Absolutely not. Last night you did not keep your promise and get my car back on time, so you are not going to use it. I almost had you arrested. Besides, we are going over to Bruce's to see their Christmas gifts." I said calmly but emphatically.

"Don't get any ideas about having me arrested, because I never will be. I will put a bullet through my head before I will ever let them take me."

She was ticked off. She was pacing around the house like a lion in a cage, with this evil look on her face. I said, "Come on Andrew, we're going over to Bruce's."

When we arrived at Bruce and Liz's, I suggested that Andrew stay all night there because of his mother's foul mood. They agreed. Andrew loved it there and was only too happy to stay there.

When I returned home, Mary asked, "Where is my son?"

"He wanted to stay with Alex and play with his Christmas stuff."

"I come home to see him and he stays over there?" she was ticked.

"He is at that age." I said. The rest of her waking hours she did not say a civil word to me.

Son Mike's kids were visiting from California and he was going to bring them over Monday morning for me to watch. Brennan, Bailey and Cameron arrived early on Monday morning.

Mary got up surprisingly early and started demanding right away, "I want my son home. Go get him."

I said, "I have to feed the kids first." I was trying to put off bringing Andrew home because I knew she was in a foul mood and would not be nice to him. My plan was to feed my grandchildren and take them all to a park and then out to lunch, so we could avoid Mary and give her a chance to cool off. I could see that was not going to work, because she was getting madder by the minute.

"Didn't you hear me? Go get him!" She ordered.

I sat the kids up at the breakfast bar with a bowl of cereal and went into my bedroom to put on my sneakers. There was no way out of this. I would have to get Andrew. Maybe I could just stay at Bruce's with the kids until she calmed down. She followed me into the bedroom and was yelling at me. I had my head down tying my shoes. She was about three feet away. "I ought to blow your fucking head off," she said. I looked up and was staring at a small gun pointed at my head. In the space of a few seconds, I had many thoughts. *My life is going to end this way. My grandkids are in the other room. Never in my life did I think that Mary would hold a gun on me. Was it loaded? Was it a real gun?* I went into my prayer mode. I was having trouble tying my shoes because my hands were shaking. My main thought was: *Stay calm or for sure she will blow you away.*

"I am going to get Andrew. Can't you see I am putting on my shoes?" I said calmly, keeping my head down, looking at my shoes and praying.

Again she said, "I could just pull this trigger and you will be history."

"Well, I'm going after Andrew," I hoped as I carefully stood up.

She clicked something on the gun and put it into her pocket. "You are lucky," she said. Didn't I know it!

At that point I was not sure we were in the clear, because Mary's style was not to let you go anywhere for fear you would call the police. I calmly walked into the kitchen where the kids were eating and said to them cheerfully, "Come on guys we are going to pick up Andrew." They did not question me or say, "We haven't finished eating." Nothing. Like little angels they got up and went to the car, which was in the garage, just out the kitchen door. They had no idea what had transpired in the bedroom. So far, so good, I thought. She was watching us with an evil eye but did not come after us. We buckled up, opened up the garage and backed out. No bullets. No Mary. As we drove down the street, I began to breathe. I could hardly drive. The little angels didn't ask a thing. They seemed to know just to ride along. Thank God Bruce and Liz only lived six blocks away.

I almost fell into Bruce's house. I went into the kitchen to tell Liz and saw that a neighbor woman was there visiting with her. I could not announce this with a neighbor there. I said hello and then found Andrew and took him into Liz and Bruce's bedroom. "Andrew, your mother just held a gun on me and I need to call the police."

"Grandma, do it before she kills someone."

I called the non-emergency police number. "I need some help. I left my house and came over to my son's house because my daughter held a gun on me and threatened to blow off my head. She is alone in our house, and I am afraid to return there."

She transferred me to an officer. "Where are you and where is your daughter?" I gave them the details. "I am first going to come over to where you are at your son's and talk to you. I will be there shortly."

Officer Brown arrived. I explained the situation to him and said, "You should know that Mary told me she would never be arrested because she would put a bullet through her head first. It's also possible she might be under the influence of drugs. I just don't know. I do know there was a change in her behavior over the past few days."

Brown excused himself and went outside where he was speaking on his walkie-talkie. He came back and said, "Mrs. Lagman, we feel we have to treat this as a self-hostage situation. If she has a gun and is under the influence of drugs, we cannot afford to take a chance that she might shoot one of our men if we try to go in there. I will stay here with you and your family and we will be in touch with what is going on over there by radio. We will do our best for a happy ending." It was then about 10:30 A.M..

We learned that the police were going to set up a command center in the church parking lot at the end of our street. They were going to evacuate part of our block. I had not lived in this house very long and knew only two neighbors. Claudia lived across the street and Joe and Lisa lived next door. They were young families. I could only imagine what kind of neighbors they thought we were. Right then it did not seem important.

Next, we heard they were sending a SWAT team out and they would be located on our neighbors' roofs and in their second story bedrooms. I had to draw a sketch of our home showing where each room was located. My mind felt detached from my body; dragged again into a horror movie which I did not want to see. My mind darted from the fear that Mary would harm herself to the fear that she would harm an officer, then to the fear that they may shoot her.

I felt grateful to the Chandler Police Department for having this officer with us, so could know what was happening. After twelve noon someone sent out for pizza. I thought Mary would be coming out of the house soon and this nightmare would all be over.

My thoughts were a jumble. *Would Mary live through this? Would she try to hurt someone? Would she shoot herself? What happened to make her resort to guns? Surely, she knew that she had gone too far this time.* I felt such relief that we had been able to get out of the house. We could have been hostages. On the other hand I felt as if I had been a hostage of Mary's for a long time.

The police team found that Mary was calling friends of hers, so they had the phone fixed so the phone was only connected to the command center. I was told that they had cut the electric power to make it more uncomfortable for her, so she would come out.

Officer Brown explained to us, "We are telling Mary to come out and lie face down on the lawn, without a weapon, and no one will get hurt." So far she was refusing to come out.

It was 4:00 P.M.. "Was Mary still moving about in there?" I asked.

"Yes, but she is refusing to budge. She has asked for a friend Denise to come to the command post to talk to her. Do you know her?"

"Yes. Denise and her husband lived next door to us at the Pointe. They were friends." I said.

"Would Denise be able to talk her out?" he asked.

"I don't know. I guess it's worth a try."

It was now early evening. I thought of our neighbors who would not be able to return home from work. The officer said that the road was blocked off. I would never be able to face our neighbors. Humility, I reminded myself. I guess I haven't developed enough of it yet.

I slipped into the bathroom and sat on the pot and put my head in my hands and cried silently. *How is this going to affect Andrew? He seems pretty calm. Has he gotten so used to violence that it feels commonplace? I doubt it.* It came to me that God gave us enough hell in our lives so we knew we did not want to go *there*. He gave us a taste of Heaven so we knew *that* is where we wanted to go. As I sat there, I wondered if Mary possibly needed an exorcism ... or was that only in the movies? She seemed to have evil spirits within her; maybe those evil spirits were drugs.

My son Mike came. Matt and Laura came. It was like a family get-together, but no one was laughing. The tension seemed to be building. Once, about 7:00 P.M. the police thought she was about to come out, then she changed her mind.

What could she be thinking? Why doesn't she just come out? I tried to put myself in her place. *What would I be thinking? I would be trying to figure out if I was going to go out there, or if I was going to put the bullet through my own head. Scary thought either way.* I knew that tragedy and success were suspended in a delicate balance.

At 9:30 P.M. Officer Brown explained to us that they felt it was necessary to put an end to the stand-off. He said they were going to shoot pepper spray cartridges into the house in different places. She will not be able to breathe and she will have to come out. You need to know that it causes damage to the house. We shoot them through windows toward a wall, where they will hit a wall and explode a fine mist of powder, which will penetrate everything in your house. Every closet, drawer, nook and cranny will have this spray in it. You will not be able to live there for several days.

"Whatever you have to do, do it," I said.

They fired nine cartridges into various windows around the house.

At 10:00 P.M. Mary came out and threw herself down on the lawn and was taken into custody. The police team needed to find the gun. They asked me where her things were. I told them, "In the garage on the west wall there is a big suitcase and three garbage bags." They found the little handgun with two live rounds in it.

How did Mary get involved with guns? There was so much that I didn't know of her life. All I knew about was her life was the life she had with us and what she told us, which wasn't much.

We were not allowed to go into the house until midnight because of the fumes and powder and then only to secure it. Even with the information given to me by Officer Brown, I was not prepared for what my home looked like when we arrived. It looked like a war zone. The garage was open and Mary's belongings were scattered all over the garage from the search for the gun. We took a quick look. It was hard to breathe in the house and our eyes were watering. This fine powder had sifted through everything and I mean *everything*. Nothing escaped that powder.

The windows and blinds were ruined where the cartridges entered. The walls had big holes where the cartridges had hit and exploded. In my bathroom the cartridge went into the huge mirror and through the glass shower door. There were piles of glass shards scattered everywhere. My beautiful new home was a shambles. I felt sick. *At least no one was hurt.* Sometimes it was hard to keep priorities straight.

My sons, their wives and Kim were a huge comfort and help. We secured the house the best we could until morning. The next morning we notified my insurance company who was very cooperative. We gathered everything out of closets and drawers—nineteen bags which either had to be laundered or cleaned. Daughters-in-law, Liz and Laura went to work on those. Those gals were lifesavers. It would have been easy for me to give up and collapse, but they kept me going and engineered the whole clean-up.

As if we were not beaten down enough, the second night that we were unable to stay at the house, someone entered my home through a back window and stole CDs, videos, Andrews Play Station game with all the controls and games, a boom box, and a radio. The insurance covered all of the home damage and theft except for the deductible and, of course, the hours and hours put in by Liz, Laura and me. The total insurance claim was over $10,000.

The toll it took on me was strange. I wasn't depressed, but I wasn't okay either. I was somewhere in limbo. I could not get past the fact that my own daughter had held a gun on me. *Did she hate me that much?* I was genuinely afraid of her now. Even after all I had been through with her, I never thought she would resort to guns. I was in a state of disbelief. *Where did she get the gun? What if she had shot me?* Talk about a wake-up call.

An unbelievable and puzzling thing: Mary totally denied that she ever held a gun on me. To this day she sticks to that story. She actually told the police that she did not hold a gun on me. I had read that people sometimes develop a type of amnesia for painful events. She was certainly having amnesia about this. If it were as painful for her to think about holding a gun on me as it was for me to experience it, then I could understand her blocking it out. Holding a gun on your own mother was beyond my ability to comprehend.

The first day that we were able to work in the house, my west neighbor Joe came over with a bouquet of flowers. I was touched. He said, "We understand what you've been through and want you to know we are here for you." My neighbor Claudia from across the street went to McDonalds and bought burgers for Liz, Laura, me and the kids while we worked to clean up the house. At least two neighbors still liked me!

To this day I don't know what the other neighbors thought. I have lived in the same house for eight years and do not know any of the other neighbors, except to say hello or wave. Even though that is the only incident that emanated from this house, they probably labeled it as a house where "major police activity took place." It seems to be human nature for most people to want to distance themselves from this kind of thing. Maybe I used to feel that way before I walked this walk. People seem to back off in distaste as if it would dirty them if they get too close. Then they could say to themselves, "That would never happen in *our* family." My heart goes out to families who live with a mentally ill person or a wayward kid who tears out their hearts and makes their lives miserable and forever labeled.

The event happened on the Monday after Christmas. I was to go to Hawaii with Steve and Kelly on Friday of that week. I wanted to cancel the trip ... did not see how I could go with all that had to be done with the house, insurance, etc. Liz and Laura insisted that I go. They said they would supervise the restoring of my house and when I returned, it would be all back to normal. What an offer. What good daughter-in-laws I had!

When I flew off to Hawaii I was not myself. I felt like a sponge that had been wrung out until you could not squeeze another drop out of it. Arriving in Hawaii, I felt as if I had left hell and traveled to Heaven.

I met Steve, Kelly and the boys at the airport in Kona. They were already there a week and met me at the plane. My grandsons Patrick and Connor placed orchid leis around my neck. It was heartwarming. They knew nothing of the incident from which I came and I couldn't bring myself to tell them. It seemed out of place in that paradise. Besides they had two friends with them. My room was an upstairs loft. We slept with the balcony door open. I could here the breakers crashing into the rocks. When I closed my eyes the noise sounded the same as lying in bed in Wisconsin when a blizzard was blowing outside.

On Wednesday morning I awakened at 6:00 A.M. and heard Steve in the dining room on his laptop. I decided I needed to tell him about what happened with

Mary before someone sent him an email about it. As I related the story to him, it had an unreal quality to it. *Had it really happened?* It seemed far away. It was easy talking to Steve. He listened and weighed everything. "Mary's in bad shape isn't she?" he said.

"Yes." I said.

"What will happen to her?" he asked.

"I am not sure. I had to write a letter to the judge asking that whatever they decided, she should not be allowed to have contact with me. I have felt for a long time that Mary was bipolar. I know she does not want to be this way."

"No contact is good. You must stick to that."

"I know that now."

Our last day in Hawaii arrived. Steve, Kelly, and boys had an early flight and I had a night flight. My intention was to go to the airport with them and read a book until flight time. When they were ready to go to the airport, they gave me an envelope with $75 in it. Kelly said, "We have rented the car for another day for you, and we have made reservations at Huggy's on the Bay for you to go to dinner. We want you to have a memorable last day in Hawaii."

It was strange being there alone. I did a little sightseeing and browsed the shops. At 5:30 I went to Huggys. They treated me like royalty. They seated me outside at a table located on a section of deck which jutted out into the bay. I would have a perfect view of the sunset. I was hoping to see the "Green Flash." I was not sure what it was, but several people had asked me if I had seen it ... supposedly a green flash that sometimes occurs as the sun sets. I ordered a mixed drink from the menu called the "Green Flash." As I sat there on this perfect evening watching the sun go down into the Pacific, I had a thought that this might be my last supper. My thought was that God must know I cannot take any more crises in my life and He would take me home. Perhaps my plane was going to crash and God wanted me to have this perfect last supper. Morbid, huh? I was not frightened by it. I took a thank you card out of my purse and wrote it to Steve and Kelly. I wanted to communicate to them the joy of the week and of this evening ... perhaps my last on earth? I mailed it before I left Kona, just in case.

It was not to be my last supper after all ... but it certainly was a healing time. I spent extra time sitting there reflecting upon what a wonderful family I had. I did not dwell upon my problems, only upon the love I felt from so many. I thought of Mary in a jail cell somewhere and knew that she must feel she was in hell. As I prayed for her I wondered if I would ever see her again.

18

Life Without Mary

The victim counselor kept me informed about what was going on in Mary's case. She was given six months in jail and after that was given house arrest. Not at our house. While one of the stipulations of her probation was that she could have no contact with me, they did not stipulate that she was not to have contact with Andrew. She called him frequently. He worried about her.

From what I knew there was no way that Mary was going to handle house arrest. The rules were too stringent for her. Later we heard that she blew the house arrest and was hiding out. I was afraid that she might try to come to our house. I checked every door and window lock every night. I had never imagined that Mary would kill me, until she held that gun on me. I realized then that one wiggle of her finger would have made the difference between life and death for me. Mary usually blamed *me* every time she got in trouble, so I figured she blamed me for her arrest this time too …

Eventually, the police caught up with Mary at a friend's house. She was arrested and given three years in prison. For the first time in twenty-five years I would not live with the thought that at any moment our lives would be interrupted by some explosive event produced and directed by Mary. While I still wasn't able to get my dreams back, I began to feel hopeful. It was a strange thing losing your dreams. It was like a nearly dead battery—it grunts and groans, but it won't ignite. Whenever a thought entered my mind about a new venture or job, I couldn't care that much about it. I functioned outwardly. I went through all the acting like my old self. I doubt anyone else knew that I had had lost my dreams. Until I lost them, I didn't realize the importance of them. I was half a person. I found when a new opportunity came my way, my attitude was generally: *Why would I do that? What difference would that make? Am I becoming a cynic?*

After Mary was out of our lives, I received a call from my friend and colleague Kathy. She was the Executive Director of a retirement community in Tucson and was also temporarily managing a community in California near San Jose. She wanted me, as a consultant, to take over her California responsibilities. She said, "I can only go back to Tucson if I can find someone who could take this project over so smoothly that the residents will barely notice. The residents really like me. You are the only one I can think of who could take over and they will hardly notice there has been a transition. I would stay for awhile during the transition to assist in the changeover."

I had hired Kathy in 1990 to be the Executive Director of the Forum at Tucson. We had worked very well together there, but had actually been friends for twenty years. She and I were close and she was aware of my home challenges, having witnessed a few of them first hand. She knew all about our struggles with Mary.

The plan was made that I would fly to San Jose every Tuesday morning and fly home on Friday evening. I would be commuting. Andrew would stay with Liz and Bruce part of the time and the rest of the time with daughter Kim who still lived with us.

Andrew was receiving a few letters from Mary in jail. They were long letters and full of apology. She was angry at me and asked how I could have said she held a gun on me. She was denying that fact, and said she would never have done that. I wondered if she had multiple personalities. Perhaps one personality held the gun on me and the other personality didn't know anything about it. I vowed that I would not write to Mary in prison and I would never take Andrew to visit her there. Nor would I send her any money. I felt she had taken enough of my money. I did not want Andrew to see his mother in prison. I did not want to write to her because I felt this emphatically: If Mary had reached the point of holding a gun on me; we must be separated for the good of both of us. I still prayed for her every day.

It was January 2000. Andrew was fourteen years old. Kim was 32. I was 61. Where had the time gone? I received a call from my old friend Elsie in Cuba City, Wisconsin, who told me that our good friend Purs Creswick had died. We had not been in communication with the Creswicks except for annual Christmas cards. I remembered all the good times we had together as couples. We had been such good friends and all of us felt the loss. The kids and I sent flowers.

A few weeks later I received a nice thank you from Ken, Purs' husband and my old boss at Southwest Health Center, in Wisconsin. In addition to thanking us for the flowers, he asked about the kids and about my job. I answered the letter, telling about my family and asking about his three daughters. At that time I was involved in leading a grief support group at my church and offered Ken some support for his grief. Thus began a correspondence which became a regular occurrence. I had worked for Ken for seven years in Cuba City, and we had become quite close. I considered him one of the best friends I ever had, as well as a great mentor for my career. That was twenty years ago.

We seemed to pick up the old friendship easily. After a few months of corresponding, I picked up the phone one evening, and it was Ken. Thus began a weekly phone conversation in addition to the letters. Then it became three times a week. Then it was a daily conversation. A few of my very close friends knew about it, but none of the kids knew. Our conversations were becoming more of a romantic nature. I had not felt this way about anyone in more years than I could remember. I was hesitant to begin a relationship with anyone considering my murky life with Mary. *Could I have a relationship? I'm not sure. Could I recapture my dreams? Could I have normalcy in my life?*

In May Ken said, "I think I would like to come and visit you in Phoenix."

"Really?" I stuttered.

"Yes, really"

"When?"

"How about June 4th? I would arrive on Thursday evening and return on Tuesday morning."

"That sounds good."

"Can you put me up?"

"Of course."

I was a wreck. I had put on weight since I left Cuba City. Would he be disappointed? He sent a photo of himself "because I want you to see how old I am," he said. Ken was sixteen years older than I. He was always a handsome, well-dressed guy who commanded respect wherever he went … professionally or socially, and he had charisma.

I had mixed emotions about Ken's visit. On the one hand I was excited about it. On the other hand I felt that it was not possible that something wonderful could happen in my life. I had been on a long and painful road and I thought it would always be that way.

Before Ken came to visit, my sister Joan and two nieces Barbara and Carolyn came to visit from Colorado and Wyoming. We always had fun when they came. We were all in the kitchen on Saturday morning when the phone rang. It was Ken. When I got off the phone, they all chimed in, "Who was that? That was a man!" My sis said, "I can tell by the way you lit up!"

So I told them about Ken. "I have not told the family yet. Maybe they won't approve. I've been very close to them … a good baby-sitter and a good grandma. They have been my life."

Jokingly Carolyn said, "What you need to do is shock them first. Then when you tell them there is a man in your life, they will think it is okay."

"What if I first tell them I am gay and then when they act shocked, I will tell them the truth, 'No, I am not gay, but there is a man in my life?'"

We giggled and decided that I would present the above scenario at Bruce and Liz's that evening at the family get-together, which they were hosting.

As Bruce was blending Margaritas, I said, "Bruce, there is something I have been meaning to tell you."

"What's that, Mom?"

"I am gay."

He did not bat an eyelash and said, "Whatever floats your boat, Mom. It's okay with me."

"Bruce! You are supposed to be shocked." I was the one shocked.

"You can't shock me, Mom."

"Bruce, I'm not gay, but there is a man in my life."

"That's okay too," he said. "Anyone we know?"

"As a matter of fact you do know him. It's Ken Creswick from Cuba City."

"That's good news!" he replied. Matt and Laura had not yet arrived, so I repeated the performance for them.

"Matt," I said, "You were not here when I made my announcement."

"What's that, Mom?"

"I told Bruce that I was gay." I waited for his response.

He too did not miss a beat. "That's okay, Mom, if it makes you happy."

"What is it with you guys? You are not even shocked! What would I have to do to shock you?"

"Nothing you could do would shock me, Mom." Matt said.

"Well, Matt, I hope you won't be disappointed, but I'm not gay. There is a man in my life!"

"That's even better. Who is it?"

"It's Ken Creswick from Cuba City"

"Mom, that's super. He's a great guy. How did all this come about?"

I related how we had begun writing after Purs died.

"By the way, he is coming to see me in June."

"Really? It sounds serious, Mom."

"I don't know," I said.

My son Mike was not at the party but he dropped by the house the next morning and I dropped the "gay bomb" on him. I almost got a shock out of him. At least he stopped chewing in midstream. I quickly told him that I was not gay and he said, "Oh, good!" When I told him about Ken, he seemed pleased and surprised.

When I told daughter Kim I did not need to shock her first. When she was a child, she had always loved Ken. She had called him "Uncle Kenny." She was obviously delighted when I told her.

I wondered what Mary's reaction would be when she heard about Ken and me. I actually did not think much about Mary during this time. I was filled with hope and I had a new spring to my walk.

I had begun my consulting in San Jose, but Kathy was still with me for the transition period, so I was able to get the time off while Ken visited. Kim and Andrew stayed elsewhere during the visit.

I met Ken's plane at the airport after trying on four different outfits to see which one made me look the slimmest. Should I wear my glasses? I could only see about five feet without them. But I did not look good in them. I decided I would just have to try to pick him out of the deplaning crowd without my glasses. I was squinting, trying to find him when he came right up and touched my shoulder, "Are you looking for someone?" I jumped.

Have you ever run into an old friend that you really liked but had not seen in a long time? That's the way it was with us. We hugged and beamed at each other. Everything was going to be fine. We went back to the house and sat on the patio with a drink and reminisced about old times. We fit together just like missing pieces of a puzzle.

On Saturday night Ken said, "Let's go to a nice restaurant. Maybe there is one that has some music?"

"There is a new place in Gilbert that is getting good reviews. They are supposed to have a jazz group." We made reservations and had a lovely dinner.

While we were eating, Ken said, "Gayle, I know I am a lot older than you, so you may not be in favor of this, but I know that I want to spend the rest of my life with you. Will you marry me?"

I was overcome with a mixture of feelings. I felt a huge amount of love for him, but I needed to level with him about the hell I had been through. Maybe then he would change his mind. "Ken, before I give you an answer, I need to tell you the hell that I have lived in and out of for the last twenty years. Then if you are still interested we can talk about it." I spent the next hour and a half giving him the detail. I did not hold anything back. I ended with the "gun event," thinking for sure that would finish off any feelings he had for me. I explained that Mary was now in prison for three years.

With tears in his eyes, he said, "I am only sorry that you had to go through that alone. You haven't changed my mind. I still want you for my wife. What do you say?"

"I say yes. I would love to be with you. What would we do about our living arrangement? All of my professional contacts are here."

"I would sell my house and move down here."

"What do you think your kids would say about that?"

"I know my kids want me to be happy."

I was pretty sure my kids would be happy about it. We were going to meet Bruce and Liz, Mike, Matt and Laura, and Kim for dinner on Sunday at a restaurant. Ken and I had not discussed when to tell the kids about our plans to be married. We were seated at a long table, with the Mike, Matt, and Bruce sitting directly across from us and their wives sitting farther down the table. Out of the clear blue, Ken made a speech.

"Matt, in the absence of your older brother Steven, you are the eldest, so I would like to address this to you." They all looked up at him. The girls were sitting at the other end of the table gabbing and were not aware of the fanfare.

"Yes, Ken?"

"Matt, I would like to ask for the hand of your mother in marriage."

The boys pretended to put there heads together in a discussion. "Do you think he can fix things?" Bruce asked.

Mike asked, "Do you suppose he could change out the garbage disposal?"

"Will he mow the lawn?" Matt asked.

Then they quickly brought their heads up and said in unison, "We approve!" They seemed genuinely happy for us. I felt ecstatic beyond words.

It was as if God had spoken to me, "You have had enough unhappiness. Now I am blessing you with someone and something very special for your life. I am giving your dreams back." I think my friends were in shock and maybe I was too. When I was first divorced, I thought I would probably get married again at some point, but I had not thought about marriage or even wanted to get married for years. I had dated and always decided I was better off single.

Ken and I were married in January. His wife Purs had been gone for one year and that was a bit soon perhaps, but at our age we did not see any sense in waiting longer. Ken was moving to Arizona and that was hard for his daughters, but they gave their blessing. We felt we had exceptional kids. All nine of our kids counting Andrew, excluding Mary, marched down the aisle ahead of us at St. Tim's and gave us away. A few close friends and lots of relatives joined us in the celebration ... one hundred of them.

I could not recall such happiness and joy. To me there was a difference between happiness and joy. I felt that happiness came from outside of you and was often short-lived. Joy was a gift from God and came from within. Joy could stay with you even through hell and high water. I now felt both.

Kim moved to an apartment and Ken and I began our life together with Andrew. While I did not think of Mary, even though she wrote regularly, I still prayed for her every night. Her letters were full of apologies and denials. She swore that she would never have used a gun on me. She admitted to heavy drug usage in her life, but did not specify a particular period of time. I felt detached from Mary, which I thought was a good thing for both of us.

I did not work the first year we were married. That was the first time I had not had some kind of job since I was twelve years old, delivering papers and baby-sitting. Ken and I took a two-month summer vacation visiting family and friends in Wisconsin.

During our first few years together we experienced several serious losses. Ken's youngest daughter Wendy died of breast cancer before her 40th birthday, leaving two boys Jake twelve, Max fourteen, and husband Charlie. It was heartbreaking.

I lost my brother Steve who had become a friend to Ken and lived down the street from us. I also lost my sister-in-law June, and my niece Marsha. One of my best friends Kathy, whom I worked with in San Jose became ill with cancer and died within six months. That hit me hard. When she was in the hospital in Scottsdale, I would visit her in the morning before work and help her to meditate. We even tried hypnosis to help her get rid of her nausea. Kathy was my closest friend to die and she was only fifty years old.

To top it off, Ken's PSA shot up and he was diagnosed with prostate cancer. He was in treatment during Wendy's illness. Our relationship was strong and we comforted each other during our losses. Ken got excellent treatment and his PSA returned to zero. We had beaten the prostate cancer, at least for the time being. We were aware when we married that we were both older and we did not know how much time we would have together. As I said to Ken, "Not even young married couples know how much time they have together." We were committed to enjoying every single moment that we had. And we did. I introduced him to Starbucks. We would go there and do a crossword puzzle. Sometimes we walked there with our two dogs. His dog was Bailey and mine was Baby. They liked each other from the beginning. We walked them every morning except Sunday. Ken was Methodist and I Catholic. Sometimes we went together to his church and then to mine. Other times he went to his and I went to mine.

Letters arrived regularly from Mary in prison. I did not want to read them, but I did. There was a change in the subject matter. They became spiritual in nature. There were a couple prison missionaries who visited Mary regularly, and she was gaining strength from them and their prayers. She was also doing a lot of reading.

In her last year there Mary asked for a little money, letters, and visits from me and from Andrew. She would tell how other inmates had TVs and visitors and she had nothing. I felt no guilt over her pleadings. I had vowed not to send her a penny after all the money I had lost because of her. I would not visit her and I would not take Andrew there to visit her. I could not bring myself to do anything to make her more comfortable there. She had chosen that avenue. Besides, I felt we needed absolute distance between us.

I became aware that Mary's brother Steve was corresponding with her. I was glad about that. It gave her family contact, and I knew Steve would see that she had money if she truly needed it. It saved me from having to have contact that I felt would not help either one of us. I had a life separate from Mary.

Ken and I refinanced the house and used some of the equity to finish paying off my credit card debt. Seven years after I had lost everything, I was finally debt clear. I often wondered if Mary realized the extent of the financial damage I had suffered from her escapades.

I had always been the kind of person that would take an awful lot from a person and keep forgiving them over and over. However, once I reached that point where I decided I was through, then I was really through. Caput. Finished. That was what happened to finally bring my first marriage to a close and that is what happened with Mary. When she held the gun on me, I was through. I no longer wanted a relationship with her. Did I still love her? Yes. I prayed that she would hate prison so much that she would never want to go back. I prayed that the life I was now living would never be dominated by Mary. I prayed that she would not become worse from her associations in prison. I prayed that she would have peace and not live in her hell anymore. I realized that Mary lived in a hell. She was suffering. She felt pain. At the time someone was inflicting pain on you it was difficult to realize that the perpetrator was in pain. In the past it had entered my mind that her life was a hell, but I could only see my own hell. Once I began to understand that she was in pain, I began to forgive her. My son Steve was a factor in getting me to see that Mary was in pain.

19

Life With A Different Mary

Oldest son Steven, the anesthesiologist, took over the "nurturing parent" role with Mary. I could not do it. He continued writing to Mary. I knew that he interceded on her behalf with the prison medical personnel to get her on medication. She was finally getting treatment for bipolar disorder ... at age 34. I guess you could say that we practically diagnosed her ourselves.

I could not help thinking that if she had been on medication, much of the violence would never have happened. Steve became her only close family person. He became her confidante and her hope. I was grateful to him. Mary related how she had become very close to Steve and he was her mentor.

As Mary's three-year sentence was nearing the end, I could no longer postpone thinking about what that might mean to all of us in the family. Steve was in Madison, Wisconsin. We all lived in Arizona. She was here. Steve and I discussed it. Steve felt Mary had changed and that the medications had helped her.

We called a family meeting. The question which we were to consider, "Would we let Mary enter into our family life again?" After much discussion, it was decided unanimously to let her back into the family, with the understanding that if there was any more violent behavior, the relationship would be over. This meant that Mary would be invited to all family get-togethers, etc. Steve was going to pay for her lodging and expenses, at least in the beginning.

It was a hard transition for Mary and me. Mary had put on lots of weight in prison by eating a high carbohydrate diet and by taking the psych meds, which were known for causing weight gain. Many of her clothes had been lost.

She had become acclimated to prison life and was seen by her mates there as a person they could lean on. Mary was a leader. If only she could lead people to good things. She related that she was strength for many women in prison. If only she could tap into that when she was released.

When Mary first got out she stayed at motels at Steve's expense. Steve would pay a week at a time. He paid for groceries, personal items, and a few clothes. I would take her to get them. I bought her a few things and brought her little "care packages." It was still a miserable existence for Mary. She was very self-conscious about her appearance. In prison when she had a toothache, they pulled the tooth. She was short on teeth. After a few weeks of motel life, Mary went to live with an old friend Anna who had two children. Steve would pay half the rent and some of the other expenses. That arrangement seemed to work well at first. We included Anna and her two girls in family gatherings.

As with all other people Mary had lived with in her lifetime, it did not work out. Mary was trying to "fix" Anna and her girls and would get very upset at them. Steve and I agreed with Mary that it was not going to work in the long run. We found an apartment house that was willing to take felons, as long as they had met the conditions of their parole. We visited second hand stores to get the bare minimums that she would need and moved her in. Mary had made a big decision:

She had finally realized that she could not live with other people. She got herself two dogs and they became her roommates.

It was only after Mary began living on her own that we began to develop a relationship for the first time in our adult lives. She needed me to take her to the store and doctor appointments. She began calling me several times throughout the day when I was home. They were often just "touch base" calls. I knew she was lonely. She seemed to be more able to share her feelings. She would talk about her feelings of loneliness and about the hurt she felt over the lost relationship with her son Andrew, who presently did not want much to do with her.

Little by little our little trips became more social. We might stop at Starbucks or stop for lunch. One day as I was sitting across from Mary at lunch, it dawned on me that we were having a peaceful and fun lunch. I was enjoying Mary as I never had. In our past life together, we had never had one lunch out together without some emotional outburst. She was now even nice to the waitresses. I began to realize that Mary was not the same person. I began to realize that we were forming a mother-daughter relationship.

Mary was seeing her sister Kim frequently. Kim would make food for her and would take her places. That was a new development—a relationship with her sister.

I did not know what the future held. I knew Mary was having an existence, not a quality life. I knew that adjustments to medication often put her into a hell where she felt such pain that I was afraid she would end it all. Steve was still her confidante and friend. He said to me, "I am glad for this time I have shared with Mary. I like her."

For the first time I could look back without pain and review Mary's life. Oh, the wonders of hindsight. Why can we see things so clearly when looking backward? When I was a teen-ager my dream was to have a happy marriage and lots of wonderful children. I came from a big, happy family. After becoming a nurse, marrying and beginning my own family, I felt as if I had the world by a string. Everything was going our way. We chose to augment the joy we felt with our four sons by adding two daughters to our family. We did not want to take babies from young childless couples, so we sought out special needs children.

As our family grew, the special needs of our daughters created a rift within our family unit. Raul and I could not agree with each other as to the handling of the problems. In our case we became supersaturated with the problems created within the family.

We both had demanding professions and five other children to parent, and we failed to nurture the marital relationship. Without realizing it our modus operandi became survival. I shuddered to think of how many families have traveled that same ground when mental illness or other behavioral challenges reared their ugly head.

When the agency found a baby girl for us, we were excited and did not ask things like: Was the mother a drug user or an alcoholic? Did the mother have psychiatric problems? If we *had* asked them, I do not know if our social worker would have known the answers. Even if we knew the mother *had* taken drugs or used alcohol during the pregnancy, I do not think it would have deterred us. We wanted that baby girl. We were young and fearless. I remember thinking, *How could we be so fortunate as to have another perfectly healthy child? It is environment that molds a child, not birth. We are excellent parents and have much to offer a daughter. If Mary had been our biological child and was born with problems, we would have worked it out.*

How did our world go topsy-turvy? Unbeknownst to us, within this beautiful new baby lay a terrible gift from her birth mother ... a damaged personality from the use of drugs and alcohol while pregnant. For years we blamed our parenting skills for her behavior. It took thirty five years, psych hospitalizations, numerous arrests, and a prison sentence before we finally got a diagnosis: Bipolar Disorder. It was then that she began to receive the proper drug therapy. I often wonder how our lives may have unfolded had we known of this problem from the very beginning.

The literature was full of case studies showing the break-up of the parental marriage where there was mental illness of one of the members. Why? Perhaps it was partly because of the intense roller coaster of highs and lows, creating unpredictability within the family. It may have been due to the fact that parents, in their desperation to find solutions, disagreed on key issues, and began to think the whole family would be better off if they parted company.

Bipolar Disorder, which was the awful birth gift in Mary's case, gave her a life of hell and became the powerful disease which changed every member of our family forever.

20

In Her Own Words

Author's Note: Mary, her son, her brothers and her sister were offered the opportunity to write here about their experiences during this time of their lives ... in their own words. Mary has two chapters and her siblings are combined in a chapter.

I am Mary Frances Lagman. My earliest memory was when I was about four years old. My mother was going to college and my sister and I went to day care. I remember my sister being afraid, and I had to comfort her. We were both adopted and were only two months and eleven days apart. I was aware then, that our family was split ... my dad seemed to favor me and my mother seemed to favor my four brothers and my sister. Even at that age I heard the arguments that my parents had, and most of them were about my being spoiled.

I remember being told I was adopted at an early age. I think I was about four. I was told that I was chosen. I didn't feel special, except when my mother told of the day she brought me home and how excited everybody was. My mother had four Cesareans and it took time to recover from them. Because I was adopted, she didn't have recovery time with me. She said she was so proud to have a daughter after having four boys. That was the only happy memory of being adopted that I recall.

I remember having a fear of abandonment when I was little. It bothered me so much that I would wake up with nightmares, begging my parents not to leave me ever. I would beg them not to die. Early on I had a desire to one day find my biological mom.

I hated the fighting over my behavior. I wanted my mother's love, but I never knew how to get it. I didn't know how to show my love. My love came out in temper tantrums or else I showed anger another way. I never knew how to express myself. If I was hurting, my father would do anything to make me happy. That usually meant buying me something. Then I would rub that in to my siblings, causing them to be angry at me. That caused a lot of problems in my family.

I felt so alone. All I had was my father. Even at that age I had the need to control. That made it hard for anyone to get along with me. At family get-togethers I made it hell for everybody. I didn't mean to. When I felt hurt I wanted to hurt back. My hurt turned into anger. That seemed to be the only way I could express myself. Most of my anger and rage was directed toward my family. I became violent. I didn't know how to express my hurt. I began to hate them and the way they made me feel.

I guess I realized something was wrong when we adopted my sister. She needed special attention. My dad didn't like that because he felt I was pushed aside. I think my family became divided at this time. It seemed to me that it was my dad and I against the rest of the family.

It was clear to me that my father wasn't fond of my sister Kim. I think he felt as if the others were pushing me aside. That is when the spoiling by my dad really started. He didn't like to see me hurt.

I felt that the relationship with my dad was good. He made everything better. I felt that our relationship came between the relationships that my brothers wanted to have with their dad. I never wanted him out of my sight.

My father was a doctor. I remember going to the hospital to wait for him to make rounds with his patients. I felt protected when I was with him. I didn't hurt. When I was around the others I never felt like I belonged. I guess they were just kids too, and they didn't know why I acted the way I did. I didn't understand all my rage and anger. I think I understood why my mother didn't like me—at least it sure felt like it. It seemed that all I heard was fighting between my parents and it always seemed to be over me.

I felt like my mother hated me. The only thing she showed me was discipline. She slapped and belted me, and put soap in my mouth. Most of this happened when my father wasn't around. He would have protected me. I hated to be alone with my mother and my siblings. I couldn't run to Dad so he could make it better.

My relationship with my mother was difficult. I do not remember a time that we got along. I always wanted to have a relationship with her. Who doesn't want to have a relationship with their mother? We both had strong personalities. Mom was always right. I soon learned that standing up for myself would do no good. So I let her tell the stories as she saw it. If I disagreed with her it turned into an argument. That is where many of our battles began.

I admit that the first time I really heard "no" and had no place to get "yes", was when we moved to Arizona. It was not easy for me to accept, and caused many fights. I felt out of place once we were in Arizona. I had no one to stand up for me, and I felt alone and hurt. Since I was able to express such a limited amount of feelings, the hurt turned into anger and the anger lead to violence. It was only a matter of time before I could not take it anymore.

My mother and I always had a communication problem. I felt this caused me to keep all my feelings inside of me. My anger would build up. We could never talk about it or resolve anything. I was often told that my feeling were wrong. It seemed that my family was concerned with the way I made *them* feel. I wanted them to acknowledge *my* pain, as well.

I think the lack of communication was our biggest problem. I take responsibility for not being able to express myself properly. I felt from a young age that my mother didn't like me. I never recall her ever saying anything nice about me. This hurt me greatly. I became violent against Mom, as well as my siblings. Words were not an option anymore.

I had explosions. I felt bad afterwards and I wished that I could have gotten my point across by verbalizing how I felt. I had way too much rage by the time I was twelve. I was aware most of the time what I was feeling, but why I could not express them, I don't know. When I look back there are many things I wish I could have changed during my growing up years. I never knew why my highs and lows were so extreme. All I knew was that I felt out of control.

No doubt I was a spoiled brat on top of the other issues I had going. My sister Kim and I played a lot. We were the same age. She was shy, small, and fragile. I bossed her around. I felt like I was her mother most of the time. She had her fair share of problems too and also kept everything inside. I felt pretty sure that my father was not very fond of her.

I remember every school year the first few days were difficult for my sister. She always cried and I would have to be taken out of my class to comfort her. It wasn't until our teenage years that she started standing up for herself. Then it was not easy for me to boss her around, so I started to beat her up too. While I was the first one to protect her, she developed a mouth on her, which made me mad. I treated her poorly then. It was hard for her to make friends. Neither one of us understood the other ones issues. We were both "drug babies," although her results were more physical. Mine were more mental. When Kim was born she had to have a lot of operations and was in foster care until the time we adopted her at age two.

Moving to Arizona was something I could not imagine. What changes were ahead of me? I had many mixed emotions about going to Arizona and leaving my dad. I realized that I was damaged by the relationship between Dad and me. Also, I did not like my dad's girlfriend. He was no longer giving me all the attention I was used to having.

We arrived in Arizona in mid-November and started our new schools. I was outgoing and it was easy for me to make friends, but for some reason I always attracted the wrong crowd.

When I was twelve years old, I was drinking quite a bit of alcohol on the weekends when I would go somewhere with my friends. Soon I tried pot, but I really didn't like it. After I had a few drinks and a hit, it always made me throw up. As a teenager I probably smoked pot a total of ten to fifteen times. During the times I was drinking I forgot about my pain. I also had a boyfriend and began having sex at twelve years of age. I indulged myself with things that made me feel good. At home I was always fighting with someone.

That is the time when my violence began with everyone. When I wasn't hitting people, I was damaging property. I don't think my mother noticed what I was doing because my brother was acting up too. My mother decided that we would buy a house and move. Once again we were starting new schools. Again I attracted the wrong crowd and was participating in drugs, sex, and getting into fights, which resulted in my being suspended from school a few times.

My violence expanded from my home. I became a bad ass kid, fighting with other kids often for no other reason than I thought they looked at me wrong. In eighth grade I moved back to Wisconsin for a little while, thinking it would mellow me out some. The kids back home in Cuba City seemed far behind what I experienced in Arizona. I had an attitude.

I remember one day getting into it with a teacher in Cuba City that nobody liked. I remembered that from when my brother had him as a teacher. I had been paying a friend some money to do my homework and hadn't had time to copy it into my own hand writing. I was confronted by this teacher. I told him off.

It was that day that I talked to some guy friends and asked them if they wanted to run away. They agreed. That night we gathered as much money as we could. My friends met me at my house around eight. We took off on foot going through corn fields. Of course, being a girl I had more things to carry. One guy had been my best friend since kindergarten and he brought one of his friends. I was getting tired and suggested we steal a vehicle. The boys were nervous. I was too, but I didn't show it. Soon we came up to this farm. It was back in the day that people left their keys in their vehicles. We hung out for awhile before I went to check if the keys were in the Blazer. They were, so we waited for an hour or two to give the people time to go to sleep, then we got into the truck and I drove off.

We didn't have a clue as to where we were going. We just headed west. We had quite the adventure. We picked up a hitch hiker who only had one leg. We felt sorry for him. We didn't take him too far, because my friend Mike noticed he had a gun. So we soon got rid of him. We were running low on money and saw this RV owned by elderly people. We intended to rob them, but instead we helped them change a tire. On the third day out we stopped at a rest stop to call home because we were very low on money. We were in Nebraska, near the Colorado border, when we were surrounded by three cop cars. We were taken to an adult jail. I don't think it hit me what I had done, until I was in a cell by myself.

They contacted our parents. We were flown back to Wisconsin after two days in jail. My dad and the other kids' parents picked us up. I remember that for the entire trip back my dad was asking "why, why, why?" When we got released, we went out to dinner. It was then I decided that I wanted to go back to Arizona … partly because I was embarrassed, and partly because nobody in Arizona would know what I had done.

My father took care of my part of the mess I made in Wisconsin. I was suppose to go back to Wisconsin another time, but one night I was out with my friends drinking and smoking cigarettes and when I returned home I was greeted by my mom. She asked to smell my breath and accused me of smoking pot. She slapped me in the face and I hit her back.

She left to call the police. That's when I noticed my older brother's cooking knives, and began to threaten my mom and my brother Bruce with them. The guest house was apart from the main house and was connected to the garage. I saw a can of gasoline in the garage and I told them I was going to blow the place up. Soon there were cops surrounding the house trying to talk me out of the room. At one point I came out to surrender and two cops came very fast towards me. I ran back in, but I had this knife with me and I nicked an officer with the knife. I ran back in and the firemen immediately sprayed their hose and cornered me.

I was arrested and went to the juvenile detention center. I don't recall how long I was there but I do remember going into the judges chambers. My mom and the judge discussed my going to a private hospital for help. It could not be court-ordered because my parents were going to have to pay, so I agreed to go voluntarily.

I was released and went home for a few days while we were waiting for a bed to open. In the early eighties a private psych hospital seemed like a popular place to send kids that misbehaved. I fit in because all of us had one thing in common, we were problem kids. There were pro and con to being there. Part of me liked being there because I fit in and could relate to others. However, I didn't like losing control and being told what to do and when to do it. My doctor put me on medication and diagnosed me with Developmental Adjustment Reaction. I was not sure what that meant.

I did not like the medication at all. I hated how low they made me feel. I soon learned how to put it under my tongue when they gave it to me and then spit it out when they were gone. Many times I was taken down by staff and injected with a tranquilizer to calm me down.

There was this therapist named Lana who took a liking to me, and even though I left Lana's unit to go to the long term section, she would go out of her way to come and see me. That made me feel special since I had never had another adult take such interest in me. I looked forward to seeing her as well. I was seeing patients come and go. Finally, I asked my mom what kind of insurance I had. She told me "lifetime." I figured I better start playing their game.

My family and I had family sessions that ended up in yelling and fighting, we never got anything resolved. Again, to me it felt as if it was how my mom saw everything. In her eyes she was always right. I used to think my mom was all for show. Mom stepped up to the plate looking like a saint for adopting such a difficult child. It seemed to me that she thought she could do no wrong. It was always my fault. Inside of me I never felt love from her. I thought she felt it was her duty as a mother to stay with me.

I was released after being there for nine months. It wasn't too long after that my mother was on a business trip. She left the car keys at home. I had them. My brother Bruce came in and woke me up for the car keys. When I told him I didn't have the keys, he spit in my face. I went nuts. We began to fight. He hit me over the head with a piece of wood from the fire place. I made it to the kitchen and got a paring knife and stabbed him in the back. I was the one who went to jail.

21

Mary's Second Chapter

After I got out things were going okay until my father came to visit. I had my permit and told him my friend had a license. She did not. I got in trouble and was grounded. That is when I came up with the idea of "Straight Talk from Teens." I envisioned this to be a program designed for helping kids by sharing my story and other stories. When I was in the hospital, we didn't trust the staff to talk to them, so we talked amongst ourselves. That was helpful. Helping others has always helped me. My friends would always come to me to talk. I passed my idea on to Lana and to two other kids whom I wanted to add to this panel. My idea would be to do some public speaking to groups of teens.

Soon the idea took off and we were doing interviews with the newspaper in preparation for our first public presentation at Arizona State University. My panel included a doctor, a few therapists, a social worker, teacher, Director of Children Youth and Families and three of us kids. It was a huge success. I was doing radio, cable shows, and more newspaper. I felt positive for the first time in my life. My life had meaning.

It wasn't long after I started Straight Talk that my father died and part of me died with him. I can't begin to tell you the pain I felt. It was like no other pain I have ever felt. It was six days before Christmas. Nothing has ever been the same since. My family knew how hard this was on me and I was supported by many people. I thought the best thing I could do for my father was jump right back into "Straight Talk." My father was so proud of me with this Straight Talk program. It was a hard time for me. I could not keep my mind off of him. Time didn't seem to heal the wounds either.

I was nominated by then Governor Bruce Babbitt for the International Youth Year Award which was to be given by William J. Bennett, Secretary of Education … and I won! I was flown to San Francisco, along with Lana and a few other people, to accept my award. Before going there I was getting strange vibes from Lana. This was confirmed on the night before my award. After drinking alcohol she proceeded to have her way sexually with me. This really screwed me up. This was my therapist, the one I trusted. The next morning she asked, "What is wrong?" I was supposed to accept this? After all, she was my mentor, and someone I could talk to about anything. Don't get me wrong, I already had sex with a female before this, and found myself attracted to females, but not Lana … she was much older than I, and I didn't look at her that way. I didn't even know she was gay. I thought she cared about me in a therapeutic way and saw my potential.

I accepted my award and flew back to Arizona. When I spoke up about Lana and talked with others, mainly her peers, they said "most people didn't see me as a sixteen year old by the way I carried myself." When I told my doctor he said, "You need to be careful what you say, because you are in the public eye." I was not willing to go to my mother. I was going through hell. Lana used to call me and ask, "Why are you fucking up things?" I began to feel very uncomfortable around her. It caused me to feel that I could not go on with "Straight Talk". Slowly it faded away. All communication with Lana ended. I was suffering and felt so alone. I would go for long drives at night just to cry because I was hurting. I would not or could not discuss this with my mother.

I felt so alone again and felt I had no one in my corner. I felt that this terrible thing that happened to me was just being accepted. I started acting up again. I went to the county hospital crisis unit because I tried to commit suicide. Anger and rage were brewing again. I turned seventeen a month after accepting my "Straight Talk" award.

It was then that I became pregnant. The pregnancy really sent my hormones out of control. Mom didn't find out until I was five months along. Prior to that, I was in denial myself. I tried to commit suicide again and had a violent outburst. I don't recall over what, but I landed in jail pregnant.

I developed a love that I had never felt before with this body growing inside of me. I felt it was a boy. I even had dreams of what he looked like and I would talk to him. I realized I was finally going to have someone that was my own flesh and blood. That was important to me. On December 6th 1986, I gave birth by caesarean to my son Andrew. He was so beautiful and I was in love with him. I didn't know how this was going to work, because I was selfish with my sleep. Mom stepped up to the plate and I felt that Andrew brought mom and me closer. This was her first grandchild.

He was such a good baby. Mom used to tell me how lucky I was. He was teething when he was born and had a full set of teeth by the time he was eight months old. He was never fussy when he was teething. His first few years were very special to me. I never thought I could love someone so much. I felt like

Mom was trying to take over, and it made me angry. When my son was about two years old, I got into cocaine and realized I had no patience to raise my son. Mom took guardianship over him and he went to live with her in Tucson. I would go down there every week, even though my cocaine habit was out of control.

I went to see a sex therapist to deal with the issues I had about Lana, since it was still bothering me. I had been headed in a new direction before the episode with Vicki. At that time I felt like I had a chance to make something out of myself. The whole time I was in therapy, I was high on cocaine. When I was partying with my friends I forgot about everything and it numbed me. It was when I was alone or coming down that I began to feel again, so I would do more drugs to forget.

It was about this time that I went searching for my biological family. Mom helped me. I knew one day I would try to find them, but I felt a real need at this time. Since Kansas had become an open adoption state, I was able to get my birth certificate in two weeks. I remember the day I got it. I was so nervous. It only took a few hours on the phone to find them. I called Wichita information and asked if there was a person and address like the one on my birth certificate. The operator said there was one, but the number was unlisted. I told the operator the situation. She said that she would call them herself and if they wanted to talk to me they would call me. Within ten minutes I heard from my biological grandmother. I was so excited to have spoken to a blood relative. I could not wait any longer. I drove to Kansas to meet them.

When I saw my biological mother for the first time I could not believe where I came from. This woman had track marks on her arms. She was a mess. It scared me, because not only did I look like her, but our personalities were identical. I was ashamed about where I came from. The whole time I was there we partied, we drank and did cocaine. I was ready to go home. I called my Mom in the wee hours of the morning and told her that she did the right thing by adopting me.

Even though my Mom and I never got along, she was a mother figure. I went back to visit my roots a few more times throughout the years until we had a big fight. My bio mother told me about how she did drugs while she was carrying me. She remarked that I didn't seem to be affected. If she only knew!

The last time I saw her, I told her that it would be my last visit. I didn't want to become my biological mother. It was powerful enough to make me stop using cocaine. I still drank from time to time.

Shortly after the first visit with my biological family, I got pregnant with my second son Adam. He was born by caesarean on February 14th 1992. Even though I knew I was not mother material, I made a promise to God, that if I got pregnant again, and it wasn't the right time, I would give the child up for adoption. I had two previous abortions after my first son Andrew was born. Having another abortion was not an option for me. The guilt I experienced from it was too much. After meeting my biological mother, I didn't view adoption as a bad thing. I carried Adam to term and loved him like I loved Andrew. I never drank or did drugs with any of my kids. I was so against it after all the problems it had caused me and my sister. I don't know how people can take that selfish risk and poison their unborn babies.

Giving up Adam was one of the hardest things I ever did. It hurt so badly. Time did not take away the pain. I would think of him daily. It was an open adoption, so I got pictures and letters from his parents. It was so painful to have a child that I could not see or touch. It made me feel as if part of my body was missing. It was an emptiness that never went away. (His adoptive parents now say that they think he is ready to see me at age fourteen).

It wasn't long after having my son Adam that my mom purchased an Interior Design business. After high school I went to school for Interior Design and Mom thought this was a good idea and something at which I would excel. I was doing pretty well for the first year of running the business. Then I started going out to happy hour with some of the other owners. I soon met Vicki, a woman with whom I became involved.

Had I not been so empty inside, I don't think I would have gotten involved with someone like her. She kept pursuing me. I was warned about her. I was told that she had many bad qualities such as alcoholism, drug addiction/dealing, gambling and violence. Even though she was someone I did not want to be around, she would not leave me alone.

Before I knew it, we were together. She began to affect me and my life. She talked me out of every dime of mine and Mom's. I felt sorry for her, but it was affecting me negatively. I was taking money out of the design business so she could gamble or buy drugs. I wasn't myself anymore. My friends and family could not believe what I was doing and why was I with such a loser.

Mom finally looked deeply into the business and saw what was going on. Once more she gave me a chance to get rid of this poison in my life, and get my life back, even after all the money I took from her. I chose Vicki. I chose Vicki and moved out. I gave up everything … my home, my business, my son, my family and most importantly myself. I became depressed and started to use drugs. She sold drugs so it was easy to get hooked fast on cocaine. The only way we made money was with the sale of drugs. Soon I was swept away into a world that was so different from what I had known all my life. Then it became drugs, gambling and violence. For about five years this was an every day experience. I wanted a way out but I didn't know how. We lost our apartment because she gambled all the money away. I moved in with Mom for awhile. I can't tell you what happened, but she kicked me out again. I moved in with my best friend Anne for a few months.

Then I moved back into my mother's house while she was consulting in another state. I cannot tell you how many times I moved in and out of Mom's during the next few years.

Then I found an opportunity to start an escort business. Unfortunately, with that business also came drugs. Soon I was selling both. This went on for a couple of years. Then the drugs began taking a toll on me. My fuse was short. People were stealing from me. I had to put a stop to it. I went to the hotel, kicked the door down, and beat up the girl who had stolen from me. I got away, but the police were looking for me. The hotel, where I was running my business, didn't know my last name. I sent some people in to grab all my belongings and I left for Las Vegas, to stay with my best friend Anne.

I would travel back and forth to make money over the next few months. By this time I was getting tired of it all. I felt like I had to show people what would happen if they didn't pay. I was told I was wanted by the Arizona police, so I never stayed too long there.

It was December 1999 ... a few days before Christmas. I went to Arizona. On Christmas Eve my family always got together. My sister's Kim's kids were coming to our house and I was not allowed to see them. The reason I could not see them was that years ago I thought some of their behavior seemed inappropriate and I took them to see my therapist who determined that they may have been molested. When I confronted Kim's in-laws, instead of being helpful, they proceeded to get an attorney. I placed the blame for the kids' behavior on them, so they became angry at me. They now had custody of my sister's kids, and they did not want me to see them. As they arrived at Mom's house, I went out through the garage and left for the evening.

That really hurt me. It was almost too much to handle. I was so tired and in so much pain I didn't know what to do. I told Mom that I was wanted by the police for a fight I had a while back, and that's why I didn't want to stay in Arizona very long. Mom let me use her car. I did not get home until morning. Mom and I differ on what happened here. She says that I was to be back by 10:30 so she could go to Mass. In my book that is not true. At any rate, when I returned to my mother's house I was greeted with "Where in the hell have you been?"

It was obvious to me that I was not allowed to feel or have feelings. I remember this day so clearly. However, you should know that my mother and I believed differently about this day. This is my version. Two things lead up to this ordeal. The first was when I arrived home and my mother yelled at me. Another was that I had given my son a bullet from my gun, and she yelled at me and said, "What kind of mother would give her son a bullet?" I knew she hated so many things about me, but on this day my having a gun and tattoos seemed to be an issue.

I was at the computer e-mailing a friend and doing laundry as my mom was going from one room to the other. She asked me, "When in the hell are you leaving?" I was waiting for her to go and pick up my son Andrew from Bruce's house, so I could spend a little time with him. Mom was waiting for my brother Mike to bring his kids for her to baby-sit, before she could pick up Andrew. We started throwing words back and forth and I remember getting up and going to her room and pointing at her and telling her I wish she was dead. I could not stand the pain anymore from this woman. I walked out and went back to the computer.

After my brother came, I think my Mom and my niece and nephew were singing and skipping on their way to the car. I thought she was going to pick up my son. I was doing laundry and I saw a police car, so I shut the garage door. Soon the phone rang and the officer told me to come outside because they needed to talk to me. Now I am thinking this had to do with the hotel incident where I kicked the door down and did some property damage. I wasn't sure how they found me, but I refused to come out. I told them if they wanted me they would have to come and get me.

This was the straw that broke the camel's back. I was ready to die. I was so tired and emotionally hurt that I didn't want to live. I had my gun and could have killed myself, but I wanted the police to do it. I kept on asking why were there. They would not say. This stand-off started at 11:00 A.M. and ended around 9:00 P.M. with five rounds of tear gas. It was not until I arrived at the police station that I learned that Mom said I put a gun to her head. I was so blown away by that. I just lost it. My Mom was cop-happy throughout my life. I was always trying to pull out the phone lines because I knew she would call them. Putting a gun to someone's head was serious. I was not on any drugs at that time. They tested me when they took me in, but I knew I did not stand a chance. My attorney was clearly not on my side. I told him he could tell the story, since he thought he knew it. When the judge asked if the gun was loaded or unloaded I turned to my attorney and asked him.

The judge was not happy with the attorney. In turn the attorney told me, "You are your worst enemy." I already knew that. The bottom line was that I didn't have the strength to fight. I never once admitted to it because it never happened. I wish it did happen, then I could justify the 2.5 years I spent in prison. I didn't go to prison right away. I got 6 months jail and three years probation. I knew I would not last long on probation, because the girl I was living with, Andrea, was Vicki's (my ex-girlfriend) niece. Drugs were a part of her life too. With my being an addict, I knew I didn't stand a chance.

I didn't have the support system that I needed, so I went to prison for 2.5 years. In prison I got myself on medication. I knew I had a lot of work ahead of me. The only reason I wanted to try was because of my oldest brother Steve. He was an anesthesiologist. He befriended me and I felt like he loved me. I truly felt like he was God-sent. I even felt that my dead father played a role in sending Steve to help me.

At this point I felt so unloved that I felt I had nothing. I didn't even want to fight. I felt my mother had stolen my son from me. There was no reason to want a better life. All I wanted was death. That's all I ever wanted, because my life was so painful. When I was in prison I prayed a lot. I knew God before. After all, He was all I had after my dad died.

In order for me to move forward, God let me know that all the things I wanted to be resolved were not going to be resolved. He let me know that I had to let it go, in order to heal. He let me know that eventually everyone would be held accountable for the things they have done wrong here on earth.

My past kept on haunting me. All the painful memories would replay over and over in my head. All my life it was emphasized about what I did to others. Never did I hear about what they did to hurt me. It was as if that was okay. It seemed that I was not supposed to have any feelings at all. All that mattered was that I had hurt others and I was going to pay for the pain I caused them.

What people do not understand is that when someone is imprisoned, whether from being a criminal or from war, the prisoner relives their life over and over. Time stops for those imprisoned. It was easy for me to recall things from my life when time was stopped.

I cannot tell you how I made my sister Kim feel, but I bet the way I treated her when we were younger really hurt her. That is all past us now. Kim has been a great help to me since I have been out of prison.

My relationship with my siblings was always difficult. My brothers Steve and Mike were good to me. I am sure they hated the problems I caused, but they never hurt me or called me names. Sometimes they would take me with them places, and I enjoyed that very much. As far as my brothers Matt and Bruce, especially Bruce, I fought with them all the time. I think they hated the fact that I took all of dad's time and also that I would rub it in when Dad gave me money or other things.

I had always known something was wrong with me. I suffered severe highs and lows throughout my life. People, mainly my family, have suffered either directly or indirectly by my hands. I have punched, hit, slapped, choked and stabbed. I have a bad temper and I know it. Being on medication and off drugs has stabilized my mood swings. However, contrary to what people think, I still *feel* all my emotions. I have been asked by Mom and others. "Did you take your medication?" when I showed an elevated emotion. The big difference between before and now is that now I *know* when something or somebody is upsetting me and I have to get away.

I have a wonderful supporter in my brother Steve. No matter what I am feeling, he is always there for me. I haven't felt this love since my father died. My brother held my hand through all of this. When I was in prison, he was there. He never judged me or looked down on me. He was very careful, I think, on how he approached me. He didn't pretend to know where I was coming from. He didn't have quick fixes or simple answers to a complex life. I really didn't expect this from him. In the beginning I thought at any moment he was going to think he had all the answers and he would advise me on what I needed to do. But the old saying, "until you walk in my shoes" is true … you could not know. He must have known just how to handle me, because I didn't take well to others' advice. He taught me how to be a better person. He gave me strength to want to change. I am still amazed at the time he makes for me. He is a busy doctor and is married with two boys, but he still makes time for me.

My life is totally different from what I used to know. I live by myself with my two dogs. It is best that way. After I got out of prison I lived with my ex-girlfriend for a little over a year. It was pure hell. I suffered through that because I was afraid of being alone. It was getting dangerous for me to be there. Some people just get under my skin. She was one of those. I had to ask her to stay out of my life because I didn't want to hurt her. The love I get from my two dogs is enough for me right now. I am going through some health issues. In addition to being bipolar, I have diabetes, osteoarthritis, and degenerative disc disease. I am not in the best condition.

I am not sure what the future holds for me. I know there is no cure for what I have. I hate waking up every day and answering to this illness. The medication I take is strong and prevents me from doing things I would like to do. It is hard living in Arizona and being on these medications. I am supposed to avoid the sun and heat, so when I have to go out I get sick. So I stay here in my apartment prison.

What can be learned by my story? I think if I had been diagnosed earlier, and if I would have had a more positive support system, things could have been different.

First off, I believe that girls or women who use drugs during their pregnancy are guilty of a great crime ... I am living proof of it. I imagine my biological mother used drugs for the same reasons I did; however, I would never have used drugs while I was pregnant with my two sons, because I knew what it did to me. My experience has taught me that no one has the right to harm their children while they are inside the womb. My bio mother took away my chance for a normal life in order to satisfy her own selfishness. I would like to see the laws changed in order to protect unborn children. Punishment should be more severe if a pregnant woman shows positive for drug usage. It is child abuse.

I used street drugs to escape the way my illness made me feel. That does not work. It made the anger and rage more intense. It will get you a cell in prison. If you are young and think drugs are the answer to your problems, think again. They are not even good band-aids. Ask yourself if you are willing to sacrifice everything ... your family, your life, your chance at happiness.

Prison was the worst and the best thing that ever happened to me. It was the best because it prepared me for the next phase of my life where I would have to go without so many things I had taken for granted. It also gave me terrible, but necessary, time to review my life and to stop denying this illness. I finally relented to take medication. It was the worst because I had to live without any family in a 6X9 cell with another person. No freedom. Prison was hell. I knew that my post-prison life was going to be difficult. The way you are treated in our society after you get out of prison is painful. I don't know where I would be without my family. I am labeled as a criminal and as someone who cannot be trusted.

I would trade this illness for anything that had an ending ... an illness that could either be cured or would kill you. I wake up every day not knowing how I will feel that day or if I will be able to get out of bed. My medications have bad side effects. I now have diabetes and degenerative disc disease, which according to what I read, may be due to the medications. I am in poor health and my activities are limited ... and I am only 38 years old.

My brother Steve supports me financially and asks so little in return. He has taught me to go outside of myself and help others whenever I can. I practice this all the time, even when I am not feeling well. I feel this is making me to be a better person, even while I am going through all this illness brings to my table. I know it is important to help people even when you have little yourself.

22

The Siblings Speak

Authors Note: Only Steve, Mike, and Bruce chose to write of their life while growing up with Mary and the family. Mary's sister Kim, brother Matt, and son Andrew chose not to write. Kim has her own story, which was going on parallel to Mary's story. Kim was also the child of a biological mother who used drugs during pregnancy. I believe that we often ignored problems which Kim was undergoing, because Mary's were more obvious and urgent.

While growing up, Matt often spoke to me of his resentment that Mary monopolized the greatest percentage of our time, attention and energy.

Mary's son Andrew, whom I have raised, is now twenty and does not have a close relationship with his mother. He has scars from the off and on relationship with Mary. When he was about ten years old, he described it to me: "It feels like my mother holds me close and I feel good, then she punches me in the belly [*figuratively speaking*] and pushes me away." I feel that their relationship may improve in the future given Mary's current drug therapy.

Mary's Brother Bruce Lagman Speaks: My name is Bruce. I am the youngest boy, two years older than Mary and Kim. My earliest recollection of Mary was seeing a sweet baby girl about two years old carrying a football. It looked huge in her tiny arms. When I looked at a photo of that later, maybe when she was seven or eight and I was nine or ten, I remember thinking, "Whatever happened to that sweet baby?" I believed at that time that she was not like other kids.

I recall occasions when we were all loaded up and ready to go somewhere such as the cottage, Dubuque, or vacation. She would lay down in front of our Ford Country Squire station wagon or behind the rear wheels, depending upon which direction we were heading, preventing us from leaving. This was a common practice. As a child there were times I wished we would just run over her. As an adult I wondered what horrible events or circumstances could cause such tragic behavior. I remember feeling guilty and very sad for Kim. It was obvious to me that

Dad seemed to favor Mary over Kim. That was hard to understand. It divided us. It created animosity toward Mary and Dad from the rest of us.

How did I feel about Mary while I was growing up? Wow. As a naturally selfish child in a houseful of children, I hated her behavior. She was famous for raining on parades and laughing at funerals, so to speak. Her birthdays were always a disaster. Christmases were usually hit and miss. Traveling in a car with Mary was like sitting next to a time bomb. You just never knew when the slightest move would set off an explosion. I didn't hate Mary, even in her glory, when things were at their worst. After all, you don't hate your sister. You love *all* family members regardless. That is what a wise mom once told me. I was angry at Mary for the impact her behavior had on the quality of my life. As an adult I was angry at how she prevented Mom from enjoying life. That was the very, very, worst part of life with Mary for me.

I was never afraid of Mary for myself. For sure, I was afraid for others. There was a time after high school when I heard that Mary was messing around with guns. That was scary. She also had some tough friends that could give you a fright. I still considered her harmless to me personally. I never thought she would stab me or anything!

As a child I never thought of Mary as having something wrong with her. I just thought she was a royal pain in the ass that made weekends a bitch and holidays stressful. As a child I thought she wanted to be miserable and her goal in life was to be mean. The older I got, the more I understood that something in her makeup was pretty fouled up. I was about thirteen when I began thinking that Mary was not like any other kid that I knew.

When I search the corners of my mind for that one family gathering, event, trip, or outing, that was not somehow fractured by Mary's behavior, I cannot find one. I am sure there must have been some. The craziness of her antics occupies so much of my memory that there is no room for memorializing the good times. Those dreams were stolen by the bad behaviors.

As a young boy I thought that something should be done about Mary's behavior. I did not think she should be allowed to be our sister until she learned how to behave. As an adult there were times when I thought and feared that a final, awful outcome would grant all of us the closure and peace we all so desperately wanted. I was relieved when she was incarcerated, because I knew for a definite while that Mom would be without the challenges of Mary's behavior. I had no idea what was wrong with Mary, so I did not know what we should do about her. It was sad to me that we did not really know what was wrong with her head or what was in her genes to cause these behaviors. I thought that she might be possessed by the devil. There were times when I thought she had been abused. I also thought she was a product of bad genes. I also thought Dad ruined her personality. I came to think that adoption was a losing proposition.

When I was sixteen and Mary was fourteen, an incident occurred that marked the end of violence between Mary and me. I think we both realized that if we ever chose to engage in battle again, one of us would die. That was not an outcome either one of us wanted. Mary and I were home from school. Katie, Matt's girl-friend, was in the back room sleeping. I know that we were arguing about the car keys which she had and I wanted. We argued. I pushed her. She went into the kitchen and got a paring knife. She had threatened me before but this was differ-ent. She pointed the knife right at me and told me she would "fucking" kill me. Instead of walking away (poor choice in hindsight) I grabbed her and threw her to the floor, pinning her left arm under my right knee. As I lifted my left leg to pin her right arm underneath, she lurched forward, swinging her arm around me, stabbing me in the back. I remember the feeling vividly. It did not hurt at first. I felt a warm sensation like warm water running down my back. It was not water. It was blood. After learning that I had been stabbed, I grabbed her arm and she released the knife. I was madder than I had ever been. I reared back and hit her with my closed fist. She lay there. She may have been out cold. Maybe she pre-tended so I would not continue to hit her.

When I stood up I felt an incredible pain up and down the side of my back. The blood had reached the bottom of my pant leg and was dripping onto the floor. I walked to the outside bedroom where Katie was sleeping and asked her to take me to the hospital. When I tried to start the Jeep, it would not start. Katie climbed in the Jeep and I pushed it out of the driveway into the street. Every time I pushed, blood gushed out of my back. We arrived at the hospital where I remained for a few days. I was lucky; she missed any vital organ, barely missing my kidney.

My friends seemed to think it was cool and crazy. It was during football season and I missed two games. Other than that I don't remember it as being a big deal. I still don't think Mary meant to stab me. She was reacting to being pinned down.

There was a remarkable peace I felt right after in the hospital. I felt there would never be another incident like that between Mary and me. We had gone too far.

When we found out Mary was pregnant, we did not think of her son as having a chance in hell to be anything but a copy of his mother … that is, until he was born.

Andrew then became a son to all of us. He was so full of energy and so pleasant. It was astonishing to me that this person Mary, with a behavior that was filled with so much hatred and anger, so much dysfunction and turmoil, could give birth to such a wonderful child. I remember thinking maybe Mary's condition was a product of her environment, not of her genetics. I have always thought of Andrew as my own child. I want Mary and Andrew to know that regardless of whatever happens, Andrew will always be cared for and loved.

When Mom came to our house after Mary had held the gun on her, I was shocked. Andrew had stayed overnight at our house because Mom said Mary was in a foul mood and was taking it out on everyone. She did not want Andrew to be a part of that. As the day wore on it was surreal. The family was all gathered there with a Chandler police officer who kept us abreast of this nearly twelve hour ordeal through his two-way radio. None of us knew how it would end. I think everyone there was flooded with fear about the outcome. When Mary was finally brought out of the house and apprehended, I could not help but wonder when all of this hell would end.

Mary's imprisonment provided peace for Mom ... and in a way, for all of us. She was not going to be showing up. Andrew was safe. Mom was safe. Mary was safe. Three years free of worry without Mary.

I had thoughts about Mary in prison. It was not enjoyable having a family member on the inside of prison, especially knowing that the person was your sister. It was during this time that Mom married an old friend of our family, Ken, and was happier than we had ever seen her. I worried that Mary would get out and somehow worm her way back into Mom's house, starting up the misery again. This time when she was released there was no way for her to go to Mom's. Mom was married and finally had a life of her own.

I think prison is largely stupid and lacks any rehabilitative qualities whatsoever. I think it is fine for those who are going to stay locked up forever. Many who are released are worse off than when they went in. They feel so tainted and worthless, because that is what the system offers. It is not surprising that a high percentage of ex-cons end up going back inside. Also, I think for Mary it was the most horrific experience of her life and she would not want to return there.

My current relationship with Mary is fairly nonexistent. We are cordial, but we do not see each other regularly. I do not go out of my way to be away from her. I don't feel there is any threat of trouble with her as we get older and as she receives treatment. Once in awhile when we are planning a family get-together, I get that old familiar "what will happen next" feeling. I often think of Mom's safety as she ages. I consider Mary's moods and the possibility of problems. I love

Mary and I wish her well. I wish for her a life that is full of normalcy without suspense and anxiety. I forgive her for all that she has done. I forgive her for the horror she put our mother through. It is what Mom would want from me. I wish for peace in our family and peace for Mary. Extended peace would be nice. It would be like a vacation.

I have concerns about Mary's physical health. I feel she is limiting her life by not caring for herself. If she were to die I would probably feel guilty about not doing more to help her. I wish Mary some good luck. Before all is said and done, I wish something very nice would happen to Mary, so she won't feel like this life was such a bad ride.

Mary's Brother Michael Lagman Speaks: I am Mike, the third from the oldest in age. My first memory of Mary was when we lived in Larned, Kansas. I remember being very excited because my parents were going to pick up my new little sister from a hospital. She was eight days old. It seemed we waited for a very long time. I was sitting on the couch when I held her for the very first time. I did not want to let her go. When they put her back in the crib, I somehow got her back out of the crib and walked into the living room with her. I remember how surprised everyone was. Apparently they were afraid I would drop her.

I felt that my relationship with Mary was close. I didn't like it when she acted out, but I never held it against her until later in life when I felt she had become a danger to herself and to all our family. I was especially upset when she acted out in front of my children.

I remember that Mary threw a major fit every Easter. It would often happen just before church. I can remember my parents trying to get her into the car. They would say in their desperation, "Mary, get in the car or we will leave you." She would get in front of the car so we could not go. I recall that holidays were often soured by major outbursts by Mary.

When I try to remember the good times with Mary, it seems they all happened when we were little. I would try to get her to laugh because I liked to hear her cackle.

Mom asked me the question "What did you think (while you were growing up) that we should do about Mary's behavior?" I didn't think in terms of what should be done about Mary. I do remember thinking that Mary should have done things to help herself. I felt she made poor choices which made her life difficult. I felt we all gave her lots of opportunity to have a better life, but she would not take advantage of them. I knew she had a lot to overcome, but others with less ability and support had overcome more obstacles. I realize that sounds judgmental. Mary herself has voiced regrets in this direction. I had no realization that she was mentally ill.

My biggest fear was that Mary would carry out her threats to kill herself or others. I remember thinking that in our country it was too easy for her to get a gun if she wanted one. When Mary held the gun on Mom, my kids were there at the house because Mom was going to watch them. When I got a call telling me about the gun and the self-hostage situation, I felt total disbelief. I also felt relief to know my kids were safe. I also felt shame and embarrassment thinking we were going to be the top story on the evening news. I felt dread as we sat around the table at Bruce's with a detective. The police radio said that the SWAT team was about to storm the house. I knew it could end badly and my sister could be dead. It was not a good night. One good thing ... we were not on the news or in the papers.

When Mary went to prison, I felt she deserved to be there. When it was talked about in the family, I felt sorry for her and realized it must be a terrible thing for her. I thought about contacting her but I never did.

How did I feel when I knew she was getting out of prison? I had mixed feelings. I hoped that prison had changed her in a positive way, but I had often heard of prison making people worse. I was worried about that. When our family voted whether to let her back into the family, I voted yes, with the stipulation that if there was any more violence, we would end our relationship with her.

Mary's Brother, Steven Lagman, M.D. Speaks: I vaguely remember Mary as a baby when she arrived at our home in Kansas. I have a vivid recollection of her in her Easter dress and bonnet, trying to find eggs in our back yard in Wisconsin. I remember her as a delicate, beautiful baby/toddler who grew to be a rebellious child. For many years I thought she was simply spoiled—that Dad gave her anything she wanted, maybe out of sheer exhaustion. I figured it might have been the only way to shut her up. I recall many outbursts of anger, but no memories of seeing her showing fear or sadness. I feel sure now that she experienced sadness and fear, but it came out as anger and rage.

I regret that I missed so much of Mary's life. I know it is a wasted exercise to regret the past, but I cannot help wondering what might have happened if I had been a brother to her when she was younger. On the other hand I don't know if I had lived enough life at that point to have had enough wisdom to know how to help her.

My early relationship with Mary was pretty distant. Much of that was due to gender and age differences. There was over seven years between us. I do not remember many conflicts with her, until she was older. It bothered me that she stressed our parents.

My take on the family unit when we were young was that there was lots of love, laughter, and a fair amount of fighting. Overall it was more happy than conflicted. Not perfect, but happy. I had the benefit of occupying the pedestal of the eldest child. My life, by design, was easier and happier, I believe. We were a busy family. Dad worked a lot at the hospital. We understood that was part of his job. We were proud of the fact that he helped save lives and made people feel better—a noble priority, we felt.

We boys played together much of the time. It wasn't always harmonious, but we kept coming back for more. It was my perception that Dad did not like my sister Kim very much. It seemed to me that Mary liked her and they played together. Mom and Dad fought frequently. Mom did most of the child raising, troubleshooting, cooking, and cleaning. I remember going to church most Sundays.

When Mom and Dad decided to get a divorce, I thought it was necessary and a positive decision. I think it was harder on the younger kids, especially Mary. I believe she blamed herself for the breakup. Our parents did not use us as pawns like I have seen in a lot of separations. I never felt like I was losing my mom or my dad. Actually, Mom and Dad seemed to get along better apart than when they were together. This divorce made sense to me even at the age of seventeen.

As far as events that I recall regarding Mary, I remember dragging Mary back into the house during one of her tantrums. She was small enough then that I could handle her physically, but boy did she put up a fight! I remember one time that she got drunk by sipping the drinks of guests at our house for a gathering of some kind. She was just a little kid. Some people thought it was funny at the time.

While I was in college Mary and friends stole a car and drove it across several states. I visited Mom on one occasion when Mary was older and staying at Mom's house. I lectured Mary that she should be treating her mother like a queen. She glared at me when I said it. It was a look of defiance that I will never forget. I remember how angry my brothers were about Mom giving Mary so many chances. Once in awhile Mary would surprise us by doing a good deed for someone. She definitely had a good side. You could not depend upon when it would show itself.

Mary's Bipolar Disorder certainly had a disruptive effect on our family, although none of us knew bipolar was what she had. We attributed her behavior to being spoiled and unable to manage when things did not go her way. As Mary and I grew older I had very little to do with her. I was becoming a doctor, getting married, and having my own family. I guess I had pretty much given up on her as a lost cause. I did not have any answers to her problems. It was easier for me to be estranged because I was two thousand miles away. I worried that she would hurt someone in the family.

During Mary's prison time we began to have our first significant relationship. I do not know why I began writing to her. She might have sent the first letter. I was pretty cautious at first. Before long I came to like her. She showed me a part of her that I had never seen before: respect, gratitude, flexibility, tolerance, ability to compromise, and a willingness to look at things from another's point of view.

We exchanged many letters while she was in prison. I would put money into her prison account so she could buy toiletries and extra food. Sometimes I felt like her lifeline. She said my letters gave her a reason to make it through the day or night. I tried to offer words of advice and encouragement—probably more than she really wanted or needed. She became a good listener. Sometimes she asked for math lessons because she was studying. I would give them to her in my letters. Through Mary's eyes I learned a lot about prison. It's an awful place which is not conducive to success following release. I hope she never goes back there.

After her release, Mary and I continued our close relationship, even though I was in Wisconsin and she was in Arizona. Life after prison was no picnic for Mary. We learned fast that hardly anyone wanted to employ a felon. It was almost impossible to get an apartment.

I have given Mary financial assistance because I want to. I think it is the right thing to do. She is my sister and my friend. I enjoy visiting with her on the phone and getting letters from her. I do not mind her venting her frustrations to me. I feel good about her helping other people. She tells me that she knows how important that is.

What have I learned from this experience? I have learned that not every problem can be fixed. When Mary brings problems to me, she is not asking me to fix them. She wants me to listen and to understand. Mary has taught me that those with Bipolar Disorder have emotions just like the rest of us. They experience hurt feelings; they feel sadness, loneliness, anger and happiness too. She helped me to understand that it is okay to have emotions, and that emoting is not always an indication of failed pharmaceutical intervention.

I think someday we will find that so-called Bipolar Disorder is not just a single entity. We may also find that some of its variants are caused by infections or a mutation or poison or something else that is either unexpected or, in retrospect, obvious. I have a sense that even the psychiatric community is perplexed. The disorder, or set of disorders, is so hard to treat. It is such a source of frustration for patients, family member and medical practitioners.

For most of my life I believed that people behaved in negative ways because of ineffective parenting or because they were too weak-minded to behave in the way that positive, successful people do. I do not believe that anymore. I think that each of us is a product not only of our environment, but of some intrinsic hard-wiring, some of which we cannot overcome without great struggle. I think this concept of human motivation eludes most of us who have, or feel like we have control of our bodies and our minds.

I have also learned that when a bipolar person attempts to self-medicate with street drugs, which is very common, it creates an ugly downward spiral that is so powerful that it affects friends and entire families. I know that Mary can now see that too.

I have learned that prison by design is an awful place, run by people who either do not give a damn or are powerless to make a difference. Through Mary's eyes I was able to see that prison is not a place of growth and preparation for return to society, but rather a heart-hardening exercise in survival. I know the transition to life on the outside was challenging for Mary, but I was so glad she was out, and I reiterate that I hope she never goes back.

I have learned that some people judge me as weak and foolish for getting involved with Mary. They might feel I am dealing with a lost cause. I understand why they may have those feelings because I myself had given up at one time—just wishing she would disappear.

Once I began to be a brother to Mary, I began to look at her differently. I also found that the more I helped her, the less dependent she was on Mom. I have seen changes in her that I never would have thought possible. She is now one of the most grateful people I know. She thanks me all the time with letters, electronic cards, conversation. She is accepting of my criticism. In the old days she simply lashed out. She now seems able to see things from someone else's perspective. Slowly she is learning to communicate feelings more constructively. I coach her that "I hate you mother f———-is much less effective than, "That hurts my feelings." She seems to understand the difference now. She is able to admit to her imperfections. I truly feel that she is sorry for all the pain she caused. She is learning not to sweat the small stuff. She cannot yet apply it consistently, but she gets the concept. I am proud of her improvements. I am not sure Mary sees how far she has come, but I do.

Most of all, I have learned that some people need help to make it in this world. I have learned that love, kindness, and patience can be the difference between life worth living and a constant longing for death. I doubt that this is exclusive to those with Bipolar Disorder.

Epilogue

Writing the book was a chance to stand outside myself and examine our life. Do I have regrets? Absolutely. My husband and I were medical people. We should have realized early on that Mary's problems were more than being strong-willed and spoiled. We got bad advice from counselors who failed to see the disorder. If we would have been able to get a diagnosis and get Mary on medications, it would have helped considerably. Our lives would have still been difficult, but I believe they would have been much better.

I wish I had realized that I was continuously angry at Mary for her behaviors. I now realize that she mistook my anger as my not loving her, and even as hating her. I failed to see that she had feelings like the rest of us. I should have realized that *all* her emotions came out in the form of anger. Did she feel too vulnerable to show love, affection, fear, hurt? If so, I missed that cue entirely.

While I have been most aware of my own hell over the years, until this book I did not have a handle on how it affected each sibling and especially Mary's child Andrew, my grandson. He has a lot of confusion, I believe. He has a conflict when it comes to getting close to his mother. I think he doesn't trust her enough for that yet. He has some anger issues too, although he clams up instead of getting it out.

I was struck, after my first read-through of the manuscript, at how blessed we were to have survived, and to be intact and still close as a family. I cannot speak for the other family members, but I can honestly say that I am a better person for having gone on this journey. I have more compassion for others' challenges and problems. I have developed a patience that I never would have had without this journey. I see that it is not the good happenings in our lives that mold our character, it is the tough ones. And I now have humility! It is a good thing to have.

What is my current relationship with Mary? It is without a doubt the best we have ever had. There have been no major problems. We can now discuss things, and if Mary gets upset, she gets over it quickly or backs off. When she gets angry at someone else, she has learned to back off and walk away.

Mary has taught me that when she calls me and is upset about something, she is not looking for me to solve the problem; she just wants me to listen. I have learned how to listen. She does not want me to criticize or to give advice. It took me over thirty years to learn how to listen to Mary.

Mary now allows me to see her pain. All the pain she caused others in our family was nothing compared to the hell that was brewing within her. She did not choose to be the way she was. She didn't understand it. She could not control it. It was a terrible and frightening thing for her. I can see that now.

When Mary was growing up and we would go out to a restaurant for dinner, I do not remember one occasion where Mary did not get upset and ruin it for the rest of us. Now we can go out for coffee, lunch, or dinner without a problem. Mary is learning to share her feelings of hurt; she is grateful for any help she receives and she shows love and affection. She is also aware of the past problems that were caused by some of the friends she brought into her life.

Currently, I am bothered by several things concerning Mary: Number one is her quality of life. She lives by herself in a less than desirable apartment complex where crime and drugs are rampant. Her two dogs are her closest loved ones. She depends upon state aid for her bipolar medications and health care. There is no care for her teeth, which are in bad shape. She is obese, diabetic and arthritic. The psych meds have many side effects, which plague her daily. Sometimes she wants to be rid of all the medications and the symptoms which they cause, but she seems to know that the symptoms from the meds are the lesser of two evils.

For many years I did not feel that I had a daughter named Mary. I felt more like I was her lion tamer. I always felt I was the scapegoat for whatever was wrong with her life. Now I feel like Mary is my daughter. I love her and I am glad for the chance to further our relationship. I received three Mothers' Day cards from her this year. She even admitted that our relationship was making progress.

I shall be eternally grateful that my son Steve has become her mentor, her father, her brother, her financier, her friend. I cannot fathom where Mary would be without him … or where I would be, for that matter. As far as my relationship with Mary, I believe that being able to right a broken relationship before one dies, is a gift from God … and to me that makes it worth all the agony.

To adoptive parents who knowingly or unknowingly have adopted babies from drug mothers: Get help and get it early.

For readers who may be going through similar challenges, I give you hope. Don't stop loving. Don't stop praying. Be happy with small triumphs. Get help early and pursue it until you are satisfied with it. It is worth it and you will become a better person … a person filled with *humility*, patience and compassion … and you will know the definition of unconditional love.

Suggested Reading

The Bipolar Disorder Survival Guide by David J. Miklowitz, PhD

An Unquiet Mind by Kay Redfield Jamison

Bipolar Disorder Demystified by Lana R. Castle

Bipolar for Dummies by Candida Fink, M.D. and Joe Kraynak

His Bright Light by Danielle Steel

A Mood Apart by Peter C. Whybrow, M.D.

978-0-595-44076-4
0-595-44076-2